PIECES *of* ME

PATRIOTISM:

My genealogical journey of the
Eastern Shore of Maryland
1632-1832

VOLUME 1

STEPHANI JULEEANA MILLER

JOA PRESS
FLORIDA

This volume is dedicated to the memory of Mary Ellen Scott nee Downes, Reginald Downes, Jean Downes, Wilson Medford Downes, Mary Grace Downes nee Acree, Mamie Thomas nee Cephas, Stevie Beulah, and Stacey Downes, who were all instrumental in helping me write this book. Although there are many other relatives who also contributed to this journey, their efforts will never be forgotten.

Contents

ACKNOWLEDGEMENTS

I would like to express my gratitude to several individuals who have helped and inspired me throughout the process of creating this book.

First and foremost, I am deeply grateful to my husband, David, who has read through early drafts, provided encouragement, and supported me every step of the way.

I also want to thank my friend, Veronica Nealy-Morris, for her unwavering support and encouragement throughout this journey.

I am grateful to my sons, David Jr. and Julian, as well as my brother, Oliver Jr., for inspiring me to write this book and acknowledge our ancestors.

Special thanks go to my parents, Oliver Sr. and Julia, without whom I would not have had the opportunity to research our ancestors.

I would also like to express my appreciation to Vella, Edwina, Rosalie, and Avis for their participation in DNA testing, and to Wanda Jackson and Dereck Beulah for their assistance in documenting my findings.

I am deeply grateful to Anita R. Henderson, who helped awaken the writer in me and suggested breaking down the book into volumes.

Finally, I would like to thank JOA Press for assisting me in bringing our American history to life on the pages of this book.

PIECES OF ME

INTRODUCTION

In January 1977, when I was a curious thirteen-year-old girl residing in San Jose California, I became fascinated by the historical fiction TV mini-series called *Roots*. This series depicted the life of Alex Haley's forefathers from their existence in Africa, their journey across the Atlantic Ocean as slaves, their enslavement, and their eventual freedom as sharecroppers. Prior to the airing of *Roots*, my family and friends would assert that they would have never been enslaved if they lived in those times, as if they had a choice in the matter. They were proud of their African heritage and often wore Dashiki shirts and learned African dances. However, they would leave out a few generations of their ancestors who were enslaved. Watching *Roots* helped me, and others understand that we shouldn't be ashamed of our African and African American ancestors who were enslaved by the citizens of the United States.

The term "slave," which has commonly been used in books, movies, and TV to describe the ancestors of African Americans, does not solely define them. My forefathers were robust and resilient individuals who survived the treacherous transatlantic slave voyages, and were repeatedly uprooted from their families, land, and culture over hundreds of years. They were subjected to inhumane treatment, and were made to work in tobacco, cotton, rice, indigo, sugar cane, and wheat fields as if they were not human beings.

This is the story of my exploration into the genealogy of my paternal ancestors from the Eastern Shore of Maryland.

When I was born, my father, Oliver Downes Sr. was a Navy sailor, and we traveled around Europe and various states in the US during my childhood. Eventually, he retired in California after serving for twenty years. Even though my father hailed from

Ridgely in Caroline County, Maryland, I did not grow up near his hometown. Many of his ancestors on both his father's and mother's sides had lived on the Eastern Shore of Maryland for over two centuries. As a child, we would visit my paternal grandparents Wilson and Mary Grace Downes once a year, mostly during vacations or to attend funerals. It was not until I was in my late teens when we moved to West Chester, Pennsylvania, which was about two hours away from Ridgely, Maryland. From then on, we frequently visited my grandparents in Ridgely. In contrast to Alex Haley, the author, my paternal ancestors only revealed a handful of oral history details to me. One of these was shared unexpectedly by my grandmother, Mary Grace Downes (nee Acree), during one of my visits to her home. She revealed that her father, William Oliver Acree, was of Cherokee Indian descent.

Previously, my grandmother and I had never engaged in such conversations. She had never shared anything about her parents, sisters, childhood, or life with my grandfather. As a typical teenager, I thought I knew everything, so when she told me about William Oliver Acree's Cherokee Indian heritage, I remarked, "Everyone claims to have a Cherokee grandmother. Because neither my father nor any of his eight siblings had mentioned anything about our Cherokee heritage to me, I dismissed my grandmother's claim. I recall telling her that having straight black hair did not necessarily imply Native American ancestry. I even suggested that she may have had a white overseer ancestor. After my response, my grandmother ended the conversation and probably believed that I was not ready to handle this information. I wondered if this was my first encounter with an ancestor urging me to uncover their story.

Once again, I had a moment where I felt an ancestor's presence when my paternal great-aunt, Deuce (Isabella Cephas), shared some unexpected information with me. At the time, I was visiting Deuce with my father's sister, Jean Downes. Jean often checked on her elderly relatives to ensure that they were well and had everything they needed, and I joined her on this particular occasion.

Unexpectedly, Aunt Deuce, whom I had never previously had a conversation with beyond exchanging greetings, looked directly at me and disclosed that her Pritchett lineage had originated from a group of white brothers who married black women. Although I wasn't sure why, I recorded her words in writing. After that day, Aunt Deuce and I never spoke again. Again, I was not ready.

I learned three more pieces of oral history regarding my ancestry: Firstly, my paternal grandmother Elma Pritchett's lineage had Native American ancestry. Secondly, my paternal grandfather's lineage, the Matthews, originated from Canada. Thirdly, my father was related to Frederick Douglass, who also hailed from the Eastern Shore. Other Eastern Shore researchers and my DNA-tested cousins Gerald Scott, Tyrone Flamer, and Ford Wilson Jr. also claim to have heard oral history linking them to Frederick Douglass. While I respect the oral history passed down through generations, I am using DNA testing and historical documents to piece together a puzzle that may or may not align with the stories passed down orally. When I reached my late thirties, I felt ready to embrace the call of finding my ancestor's stories. However, most of my older family members had already passed away by then. I focused on researching my maternal side during this period. It wasn't until my early forties that I shifted my attention to my paternal lineage. Unfortunately, the only remaining ancestors were my father and his siblings, who could only provide information about their grandparents. I had no diaries, Bibles, or oral histories to guide me, and I had to start from scratch.

With the help of my cousin Dedra Downes-Hicks, who resides on the Eastern Shore, I conducted extensive research on my paternal ancestry by visiting local courthouses, libraries, the National Archive, cemeteries, and online genealogy websites such as Ancestry.com and Family Search. Dedra's Downes family from Greensboro, Maryland had been told that they were not related to my Ridgely's Downes family, and they were not even aware of each other's existence despite being only five miles apart. However, when Dedra and I compared our family trees, we discovered that we shared a second great-grandfather, Wilson Downes, born in 1828. Oliver Downes Sr., my father, not only shared DNA with Dedra on her paternal side but also with her maternal side and her husband, highlighting the importance of testing as many family members as possible. In my quest to trace my ancestors, I found DNA testing to be extremely useful. I convinced twelve family members, including myself, to undergo DNA testing, and this provided me with valuable information. I have also connected with many of my DNA-tested cousins both in person and online. In addition, I attended genealogy classes and conferences and organized family reunions. My relatives repeatedly inquired about when I would compile my findings into a book. However, since I believe I will never fully complete my research on my father's ancestry, I have decided to compile what I have discovered so far and divide it into several volumes. This will serve as a starting point for other researchers who wish to delve deeper into our family's lineage. This is the first volume of my journey to trace the ancestry of my father, Oliver Downes Sr., in the Eastern Shores of Maryland.

I am ready!

"Genes are like the story, and DNA is the language that the story is written in."

- Sam Kean

PIECES OF ME

Chapter 1

TOOLS OF THE TRADE

To start your family history, begin by recording what you know about yourself, parents, siblings, and grandparents, and then work your way back in your family tree. Obtain birth, marriage, and death certificates, as well as other records such as wills, deeds, census records, and tax lists. These records can be found in courthouses, state archives, old church records, and newspaper archives. However, many of the oldest courthouses were destroyed during the Revolutionary War and Civil War, so it may be difficult to prove every ancestor in every branch of your family through documentation alone.

If there are no lineage documents available, ancestors can be verified using proof arguments and case studies. It is recommended to maintain a research log to track the search locations and outcomes. Based on personal experience, sometimes one starts searching for one ancestor and ends up discovering another one, which can distract from the original search. Therefore, it's essential to document all leads to avoid confusion later on. Good documentation simplifies the process of comparing and contrasting sources. This makes it easier to judge source reliability.

Creating a timeline for your ancestors is recommended. If there are oral stories available, it is important to check if they align with your ancestor's timeline before confirming them.

DNA TESTING

Genealogy research has been enhanced significantly for me through DNA testing. The use of genetic testing kits has allowed me to discover my ancestors and learn about my family heritage. Our existence is the result of the genes passed down to us through generations, and if any of our ancestors were missing, we would not exist today. I utilized two DNA testing companies, namely 23andme and AncestryDNA, which offer autosomal tests capable of identifying relations up to five or six generations back. It is possible to have no shared DNA with second cousins or more distant relatives, but it is important to note that they are still considered cousins. The testing process generates ethnicity reports, and the companies continue to search for DNA matches as more people participate in the testing, whom I refer to as my DNA-tested cousins in this book. If you share a significant amount of DNA with another tester, it is assumed that both of you have a common ancestor. This feature can be beneficial if you are constructing a family tree or searching for unknown relatives.

How much DNA do I Receive from each Generation?

Generation	%DNA
Parents	50
Grandparents	25
Great-grandparents	12.5
Great-great-grandparents	6.25
Great-great-great-grandparents	3.125

DNA RESULTS

My father and his sisters, Vella, Edwina, and Rosalie, underwent DNA testing with AncestryDNA and 23andMe. All four siblings share the same parents. Regrettably, Mary Ellen, the youngest sibling, passed away before being able to undergo the DNA test. Nonetheless, Avis Schwartz, her daughter, was willing to take the test, which will provide a quarter of the DNA from each maternal grandparent. An autosomal DNA test is used to identify relatives such as siblings, first cousins, second cousins, and the majority of third cousins. This type of DNA test is utilized in AncestryDNA and 23andMe. While the likelihood of discovering more distant relatives may be lower, it is still possible to locate even a tenth cousin. The results of the autosomal DNA test reveal ethnicity estimates and the migration patterns of ancestors. As a genealogist, I make it clear to my clients that siblings can have different DNA, even if they have the same parents.The reason for the varying DNA among siblings despite having the same parents is due to the random assortment of their chromosomes, which results in full siblings sharing approximately 50% of their DNA. I used the illustration of an eight-color saltshaker to explain how DNA is inherited. The shaker is filled with four different colored grains from your mother and four other different colored grains from your father, making up 100% of the shaker's content. When you pour the shaker onto your brother, he will receive 50% of the grains from your mother and 50% from your father. The same applies to you. However, due to recombination, you and your brother will not inherit the same exact 50% "salt grains" from each parent. For instance, your brother might inherit the cleft chin DNA from your mother's paternal grandfather, which you did not inherit. Due to recombination you did not pick up that DNA "grain of salt" from your mother. So, that is why it is important to test as many family members to assist with your research. Since you and your brother will have varying DNA-tested cousins, it could lead to the discovery of different ancestry lineages for each of you.

DNA testing confirms a relationship but does not invalidate one. For instance, the DNA cousins that appear in my Aunt Rosalie's test results may differ from those in my father's results, but they are still considered his cousins. The only difference is that my father did not inherit the particular DNA segments that his sisters share with those DNA-tested cousins. Each sibling has a distinct ethnicity breakdown determined by the DNA they inherit, which could be traced back to ancestors from 500 to 1000 years ago.

Tool notes: Collect any documents or photographs you have, such as birth certificates, marriage licenses, or family Bibles. Interview relatives: Talk to your older relatives and ask them to share their memories and stories about the family. Record the interviews or take detailed notes. Ask if they have any old photographs or documents that you can copy or scan. Organize your information: Keep track of your research in a pedigree chart or family tree. Use software or online tools to create a digital family tree that can be easily updated and shared. Research online: Many genealogy websites offer access to historical records and other resources. Some popular sites include Ancestry.com, FamilySearch.org, and MyHeritage.com. You can search for census records, immigration records, military records, and more. DNA testing can provide clues about your ancestry and help you connect with genetic cousins. There are several companies that offer DNA testing, such as AncestryDNA, 23andMe, and MyHeritageDNA.

Figure 1 Oliver Downes Sr., circa approximately 1956

Oliver Downes Sr.'s Ancestry.com DNA Results

With more countries contributing to the DNA pool, more exact readings of the DNA will continue to update.

Ethnicity Estimate

Updated current ethnicity estimate was calculated June 2022

Cameroon, Congo & Western Bantu Peoples	26%
Nigeria	18%
England & Northwestern Europe	26%
Benin & Togo	9%
Côte d'Ivoire & Ghana	6%

Senegal	5%
Mali	5%
Ireland	2%
Eastern Bantu Peoples	1%
Central Asia-South	1%
Scotland	1%

Figure 2. Edwina Downes, circa 2021

Edwina Downes 23andme DNA Results

Current ethnicity estimate was calculated July 2021.

SUB-SAHARAN AFRICAN   **Total: 67.9%**

West African

Nigerian

27.9%   Ghanaian, Liberian & Sierra Leonean

12.%   Senegambian & Guinean

4.5%   Broadly West African

6.2%

Congolese & Southern East African   16.9%

Broadly Sub-Saharan African   0.4%
0.4%

EUROPEAN   **Total:** 31.0%

Northwestern European   29.3%

Northwestern Europeans are represented by people from as far west as Ireland, as far north as Norway, as far east as Finland, and as far south as France.

Southern European

Greek & Balkan   1.2%

Spanish & Portuguese   0.4%

Broadly Southern European   0.3%

Broadly European   0.1%

Chinese & Southeast Asian   0.6%
Indonesian, Thai, Khmer & Myanmar   0.6%

Central & South Asian

Bengali & Northeast Indian   0.1%
Southern Indian & Sri Lankan   0.1%

Figure 3. Rosalie Downes, circa 2012

Rosalie Downes Ancestry DNA Results

Ethnicity Estimate   Current ethnicity estimate calculated 2022

Cameroon, Congo & Western Bantu Peoples	30%
England & Northwestern Europe	21%
Nigeria	15%
Benin & Togo	9%
Côte d'Ivoire & Ghana	10%
Senegal	4%
Mali	2%
Nigeria-East Central	2%
Scotland	2%
Ireland	2%
Central Asia-South	1%
Greece & Albania	1%
Wales	1%

Figure 4. Vella Downes, circa 2019

Vella Downes Ancestry DNA Results

Ethnicity Estimate   Current ethnicity estimate calculated 2022

Cameroon, Congo & Western Bantu Peoples	28%
England & Northwestern Europe	26%
Nigeria	15%
Benin & Togo	13%
Mali	5%
Côte d'Ivoire & Ghana	4%
Senegal	3%
Nigeria-East Central	2%
Khoisan, Aka & Mbuti Peoples	1%
Norway	1%
Spain	1%
Ireland	1%

Figure 5. Avis Scott-Schwartz, circa 2020

Avis Scott-Schwartz Ancestry DNA Result

Ethnicity Estimate Current ethnicity estimate calculated 2022

	Total	Maternal (Mary Ellen)
Nigeria	34%	18%
Mali	14%	0%
England & Northwestern Europe	13%	10%
Ivory Coast & Ghana	9%	9%
Scotland	7%	0%
Benin & Togo	4%	4%
Nigeria—East Central	4%	0%
Cameroon, Congo & Western Bantu Peoples	4%	3%
Ireland	4%	2%
Senegal	2%	2%
Sweden & Denmark	2%	0%
Norway	2%	2%
Greece & Albania	1%	1%

The Ancestry timeline is a feature of 23andme DNA testing. The following results pertain to Edwina, Oliver's sister.

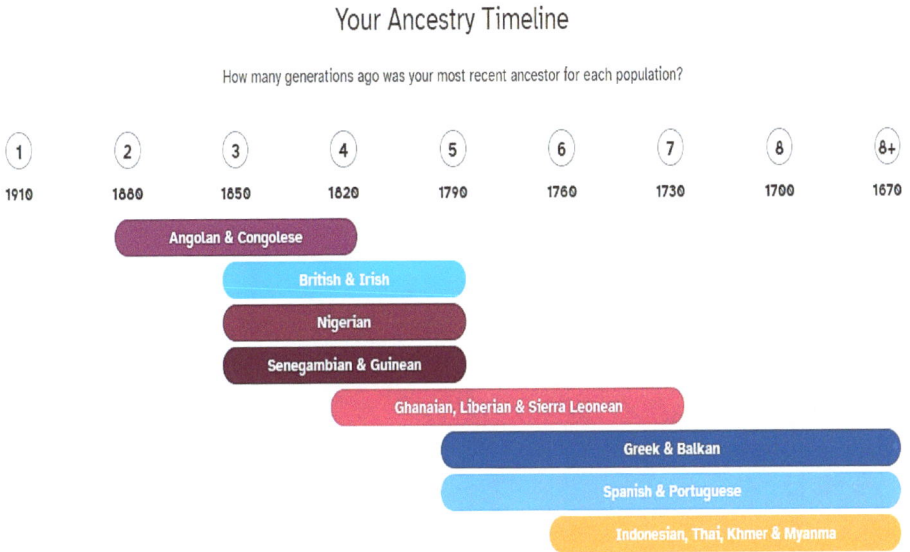

Your Ancestry Timeline

How many generations ago was your most recent ancestor for each population?

1	2	3	4	5	6	7	8	8+
1910	1880	1850	1820	1790	1760	1730	1700	1670

Angolan & Congolese

British & Irish

Nigerian

Senegambian & Guinean

Ghanaian, Liberian & Sierra Leonean

Greek & Balkan

Spanish & Portuguese

Indonesian, Thai, Khmer & Myanma

Edwina most likely had a second-great-grandparent who was 100% Angolan & Congolese. This person was born between 1820 and 1880.[i]

How many Oliver Downes Sr. Ancestors are there?

The following chart shows that Oliver could have as many as 64 potential ancestors in his 4th great-grandparents range alone. When factoring in all possible ancestors from the 8th great-grandparents to grandparent range, the number could reach as high as 2044. However, it's important to note that these numbers represent possibilities, as individuals may have double roles in their family tree. For instance, if two 2nd great-grandparents were first cousins who married, they would share the same grandparents in their lineage.

During the time period covered in this volume (1632-1832), the majority of Oliver's ancestors lived in the Eastern Shore Maryland. It is probable that there were instances of consanguineous marriages, also known as marriages between blood relatives. With limited information, I was able to find some of Oliver's ancestors through census and death certificates, but the trail only went back to approximately 1830. However, through DNA testing, I was able to trace his lineage back to the 1700s. It's remarkable to consider what Oliver's ancestors had to endure between 1632 and 1832 in order for him to exist today.

For Oliver to be born, he needed:

2 parents

4 grandparents

8 great-grandparents

16 second great-grandparents

32 third great-grandparents

64 fourth great-grandparents

128 fifth great-grandparents

256 sixth great-grandparents

512 seventh great-grandparents

1024 eighth great-grandparents

Genealogists typically use two primary forms: the ancestor chart and the family group sheet. You can easily find blank versions of these forms on the internet. An ancestor chart provides an index of your family tree and lists the names and dates of you, your parents, grandparents, and so on. I used an Ahnentafel chart to arrange the ancestors of Oliver Downes Sr.

Ahnentafel Chart

The term "ahnentafel" is derived from two German words: "ahnen" which means "ancestor" in English, and "tafel" which means "table" in English. An ahnentafel chart is essentially a pedigree chart that begins with you as the first person listed, and includes your parents, grandparents, and so on in a direct matrilineal and patrilineal ancestral line. Siblings, uncles, aunts, cousins, and other relatives are not included on this chart. In this case, the chart starts with my father, Oliver Downes Sr. The starting person will always be number 1, no matter if you are male or female. Your father will be number 2, and your mother will be number 3. Then the next generation, the paternal grandparents come first, and then the maternal grandparents.

1. Multiply any ahnentafel number by 2 and you have the ahnentafel number for that person's father. Add one to the father's number to find the same person's mother. For example, the parents of #6 are #12 and #13.
2. All even numbers are men, and all odd numbers are women.
3. Spouses are consecutive numbered pairs, with the husband having the lower number of the two numbers. For example, the husband of #11 is #10.
4. The ahnentafel number at the beginning of each generation is equal to the number of persons in that generation. That is, the 4th generation in the chart starts at number 8 and has 8 possible members.
5. Of all of the numbers in any one generation, the first half of the numbers are on the paternal side and the second half are on the maternal side.

The ahnentafel chart may not include all possible numbers for each generation, as some ancestors may be unknown or not yet proven. Additionally, there may be discrepancies in birth and death dates for certain ancestors, and various documents may list different dates. In creating the chart, I chose the best available dates at the time.

Generation 1

1. **Oliver Downes Sr.** born in Ridgely, Maryland, United States.

Generation 2   Parents

2. **Wilson M. Downes**: Born: September 28, 1909, in Ridgley, Caroline County Maryland, USA.
Died: March 27, 2005, in Easton, Talbot, Maryland, USA.

3. **Mary Grace Acree**: Born 13 Aug 1911, in Ridgely, Caroline, Maryland, USA.
Died 21 Jul 1982, in Easton, Talbot, Maryland, USA.

Generation 3   Grandparents

4. **Everett Percy Downes**: Born 2 Oct 1888, in Maryland, USA.
Died 30 Dec 1960, in Philadelphia, Pennsylvania, USA.

5. **Mamie Cephas**: Born 14 Jul 1890, in Ridgley, Caroline County, Maryland, USA.
Died 2 Jan 1983, in Ridgely, Caroline, Maryland, USA.

6. **William Oliver Acree**: Born 11 Mar 1884, in Denton, Maryland, USA.
Died 11 Feb 1940, in Denton,

Caroline, Maryland, USA.

7. **Cora Flamer**: Born 12 May 1892, in Maryland, USA.
Died 19 Jul 1972, in Denton, Caroline, Maryland, USA.

<u>Generation 4</u>   **Great-grandparents**

8. **German Empire Downes**: Born 1860, in Boonsboro, Caroline County, Maryland, USA.
Died 23 Oct 1919, in Easton, Caroline County, Maryland, USA.

9. **Laura Virginia Matthews**: Born 2 Jan 1867, in Greensboro, Caroline, Maryland USA.
Died 30 Jun 1948, in Philadelphia, Philadelphia, Pennsylvania, USA.

10. **William Cephas**: Born Jan 1862, in Dorchester County, Maryland, USA.
Died after 1910.

11. **Elma Pritchett**: Born Apr 1869, in Ridgley, Maryland, USA.
Died in Ridgley, Caroline County, Maryland, USA.

12. **Robert D. Acree**: Born 5 Apr 1845, in King and Queen County, Virginia, USA.
Died 18 Apr 1917, in Ridgely, Caroline County, Maryland, USA.

13. Mary J. Johns: Born Apr 1858, in Maryland, USA.
Died 9 Jun 1911, in Caroline County,
Maryland, USA.

14. James Flamer: Born 1842, in Hillsboro, Caroline,
Maryland, USA.
Died 18 Aug 1922, in Denton,
Caroline, Maryland, USA.

15. Sarah R. Sparks: Born 1843, in Maryland, USA.

Generation 5   2nd Great-grandparents

16. Wilson Downes: Born about 1830, in Maryland, USA.

17. Elizabeth Unknown: Born about 1835, in Maryland, USA.

18. Robert M. Matthews: Born 1837, in Caroline County,
Maryland, USA.
Died 3 Jan 1888, in Greensboro,
Caroline County, Maryland, USA.

19. Henrietta Lockerman: Born about 1844, in Maryland, USA.
Died 26 Jul 1934, in Philadelphia,
Pennsylvania, USA.

20. Joseph Cephas: Born about 1819, in Maryland, USA.
Died in Maryland, USA.

21. Eliza Unknown: Born in Maryland, USA.

22. Medford Edward Pritchett: Born 1833, in Hillsborough,
Caroline County, Maryland,
USA.
Died 12 Jan 1917, in Caroline,
Maryland, USA.

23. Mary Adeline Clark: Born Aug 1842, in Caroline County, Maryland, USA.
Died 24 Jun 1902, in Caroline County, Maryland, USA.

24. Ruffin Acree: Born about 1826, in King and Queen, Virginia, USA.
Died in King and Queen County, Virginia, USA.

25. Peggy Ann Fortune: Born about 1831, in King and Queen County, Virginia, USA.
Died in King and Queen County, Virginia, USA.

26. Matthew Johns: Born 1820, in Maryland, USA.
Died in Maryland, USA.

27. Mary J. Homer: Born about 1830, in Maryland, USA.
Died in Maryland, USA.

28. Joseph Flamer: Born about 1800, in Maryland, USA.
Died in Caroline, Maryland, USA.

29. Loretta Turner: Born about 1815, in Maryland, USA.
Died in Maryland, USA.

30. John Sparks: Born about 1814, in Maryland, USA.

31. Unknown

Generation 6   **3rd Great-grandparents (26 unknown persons)**

32. Benjamin Downes: (possible) Born 1785, in Maryland, USA.

33. Unknown

34. Unknown

35. Unknown

36. Joseph Matthews: Born 1806, in Maryland, USA.

37. Henrietta Wyatt: Born 1804, in Maryland, USA.

38. John Lockerman   Born 1802, in Caroline County, Maryland, USA.

39. Sarah Deshields (Maybe) Born 1818, in Maryland, USA.

40. Josephus Cephas: Born about 1790, in Maryland, USA.

41. Unknown

42. Unknown

43. Unknown

44. Samuel Pritchett: Born 1785, in Maryland, Caroline, Maryland, USA.
Died in Maryland, Caroline, Maryland, USA.

45. Serena Due: Born about 1810, in Maryland, USA.
Died aft 1870, in Caroline County, Maryland, USA.

46. Nathan Arthur Clark: Born about 1804, in Maryland, USA.
Died in Maryland, USA.

47. Mary Cooper: Born about 1806, in Maryland, USA.
Died in Maryland, USA.

48. Major Acree: Born 1780, in Virginia, USA.
Died before 1850, in Virginia, USA.

49. Nancy Carter: Born 1780, in Virginia, USA.

50. Taliaferro Fortune   Born about 1808, in Virginia, USA.

51. Mary

52. Unknown

53. to 62 Unknown

63. Matilda "Tilda" Sparks: Born about 1786, in Maryland.

Generation 7   4th Great-grandparents (60 unknown persons)

64. Unknown

74. Noah Wyatt (Possibility).   Born about 1760, in Maryland, USA.

75. Unknown

76. Allen Lockerman   Born 1770, in Maryland, USA.
Died 1 Jan 1856, in Caroline County, Maryland, USA.

77. Lydia Talbot   Born 1776, in Maryland USA.

90. James Due: Born about 1758, in Maryland, USA.
Died 4 Feb 1832, in Caroline County, Maryland, USA.

94. John Cooper: Born about 1770.

99. Rachael Carter:

101. Polly Fortune	Born about 1778, in Virginia, USA.

Generation 8   5th Great-grandparents

128. Unknown

148. Thomas Wyatt: Born about 1700, in Queen Anne's,

Maryland USA.

Humphrey Fortune	Born 1745, in Essex County, Virginia, USA. Died 1820, in St. Anne's Parish, Essex, Virginia, USA.
Owen Stanley	Born 1794, in Reading, Berkshire, England. Died 21 Feb 1860, in Dayton, Montgomery, Ohio, USA.
Harriet Wharton	Born 3 Jun 1794, Plymouth, Devon, England. Died 30 Aug 1857, in Dayton, Montgomery, Ohio, USA.

Generation 9   6th Great-grandparents

258. Unknown

Sarah Fortune:	Born 1715.

Generation 10   7th Great-grandparents

528. Unknown

Fortune Game Magee: Born 1687.

<u>**Generation 11**</u>   **8th Great-grandparents**

1144. Unknown

Sambo Game   Born 1670, in Africa.
Died 1734, USA.

Maudlin Magee   Born 1665, in Belfast, Northern
Ireland, United Kingdom. Died
1691, in Somerset,
Maryland, United States.

The third generation and beyond in Oliver's family tree has a significant number of unknown ancestors and histories. Additionally, ancestors listed in the fifth great-grandparent range and beyond are speculative and lack documented proof.

Tool Notes: The core of your research is about finding records that show vital events. Vital events: Birth, marriage, divorce, and death. Documents: Census records, birth certificates, marriage registration/license, county courthouse registers, newspaper notices, cemetery headstones, family Bibles, funeral obituaries, church records, original Social Security application, and institutional records (schools, prisons, hospitals, military, and company records).

"Genealogical trees do not flourish
among slaves."

-Frederick Douglass
Quote from the book *My Bondage and My
Freedom, 1855*

.

Chapter 2

Fatherland and Motherland

Oliver Downes Sr.'s genetic makeup is primarily composed of 70% Sub-Saharan African DNA, which refers to all African countries except the five Arab states of North Africa (Morocco, Algeria, Tunisia, Libya, Egypt) and the Sudan. It is likely that the majority of Oliver's African ancestors were brought to North America through the transatlantic slave trade. His DNA can trace his African ancestry back to West Africa, including present-day Nigeria, Republic of Cameroon, the Republic of the Congo, Côte d'Ivoire, Ghana, Senegal, Mali, Benin, and Togo.In Africa, these people identified as Mandingas, Bambara, Jolofs, Fulas, Fon, Yoruba, Edo, or Igbos, but on their arrival in Maryland they became "Negroes."[ii]

By using DNA testing of Oliver and his siblings, I was able to determine their paternal and maternal haplogroups which helped identify their fatherland and motherland. A haplogroup is a genetic population group that shares a common ancestor through either the patrilineal or matrilineal line. This means that for centuries, the father-to-son and mother-to-daughter lineages have a unique genetic marker called a haplogroup.Oliver Downes's paternal haplogroup is E-M4254, which is a subgroup of E-M180. His fatherland is Africa. If there has been no event of misattributed paternity in the Downes family, then Wilson Downes (Oliver's father) and Percy Downes (known paternal grandfather) should have the same paternal haplogroup E-M4254. Similarly, Oliver's son (Oliver Jr.) and his grandsons (Pierre and Marcus) should also have the same paternal haplogroup. According to 23andme, Oliver and Pharaoh Ramesses III share an ancient paternal-line ancestor who probably lived in north Africa or western Asia.[iii] My sons, David Jr. and Jullian, would have the same paternal haplgroup as their father David's paternal haplogroup, "E-M34, which is prevalent among Ashkenazi and Sephardic Jews, as well as among Ethiopians."[iv] Oliver's paternal haplogroup, "E-M4254 is seen at moderate frequencies on the Bahamian islands of Abaco, Eleuthra, Exuma, Grand Bahama, and New Providence.[v]

"Slaveholders in Maryland learned about the concept of slavery from Caribbean societies where they did business, where enslaved people had no legal rights. The children of enslaved women were also forced into slavery permanently. With no rights to property, or to their own names, or to families, enslaved persons could be given, sold, and rented out, much like livestock."[vi] It is possible that some of Oliver's ancestors were first taken to Barbados and the Bahamas, where they were "seasoned" in the ways of slavery, before being transported to Maryland.

One of Oliver's cousins from 23andme who has the same paternal haplogroup E-M4254 is a man from Africa with 100% African ancestry. The daughter of this cousin confirmed that her father is from Danane in the Man region of Côte d'Ivoire, Africa. This information suggests that Oliver's fatherland may be a Mandinka/Manlinke village similar to the ancestral village of Alex Haley's ancestor Kunta Kinte. The Mandinka are believed to be descendants of the great Mali Empire that thrived in West Africa from the 13th to the 16th century. "Beginning in the 16th century, as many as a third of the Mandinka population were enslaved and shipped to the Americas; therefore a sizable portion of the African-Americans in the United States are descended from the Mandinka people.[vii] Oliver's maternal haplogroup is L3f1b4a, which is associated with the Yoruba and Fulani people. It can be assumed that Oliver's mother, Mary Grace Acree, and maternal grandmother, Cora Flamer, share the same haplogroup. Additionally, Oliver's sisters and their daughters should also have this maternal haplogroup. It is important to note that Americans with African ancestry are not solely made up of one ethnic group based on their maternal and paternal haplogroups. Other African lineages can be found in the direct ancestors of Oliver, including the wife of his paternal grandfather and the husband of his maternal grandmother.

"I am an Eastern Shoreman, with all that name implies. Eastern Shore corn and Eastern Shore pork gave me my muscle. I love Maryland and the Eastern Shore!" he proclaimed proudly to an 1877 audience."

- Frederick Douglass

Chapter 3

Eastern Shore Maryland

The Eastern Shore, located on the east side of Chesapeake Bay, is a beautiful region that produces a large quantity of seafood, such as oysters, crabs, clams, and fin fish. It is composed of nine counties: Caroline, Cecil, Dorchester, Kent, Queen Anne's, Somerset, Talbot, Wicomico, and Worcester, and is known for its vast farmland, dense forests, and swamp-like tidal marshes. It was also the ancestral home of Oliver Downes Sr.'s ancestors, and many of the original settlers were Quakers who sought refuge from persecution.

Timeline of the origin of Eastern Shore Maryland

1632 King Charles granted the charter for the colony of Maryland.

1634 "The *Ark* and the *Dove* Ship brought the first settlers to Maryland. Mathias de Sousa was Maryland's first indentured that had African ancestry that arrive on the Ark."[viii]

1642 "Mathias de Sousa was the first man with African ancestry to serve in the colonial Maryland legislature." [ix]

1706 Queen Anne's County was organized under a sheriff, bounded by Talbot, Kent, and Dorchester counties.

1773 A part of Queen Anne's County, together with a part of Dorchester County, was taken to form Caroline County.

1784 Hillsboro was a rural community located on the eastern side of Tuckahoe Creek, where Caroline County borders Talbot and Queen Anne's Counties. The first settlers were tobacco planters, and after the Revolutionary War, the western part of Hillsboro was inherited by Elizabeth Baynard Downes and her husband Philemon, who sold some town lots on Main Street. The eastern part of Hillsboro was owned by John Hardcastle, who also sold some lots on his part of Main Street. By about thirty years, the property owners were farmers, laborers, and businesspeople such as coachmakers, blacksmiths, joiners, and tailors[x]. The Eastern Shore Maryland, particularly the town of Hillsboro and its surrounding areas, was a significant place for Frederick Douglass and many of Oliver Downes Sr.'s ancestors. Frederick Douglass said in his book *Narrative of the Life of Frederick Douglass, An American Slave*, that he was "born in Tuckahoe, near Hillsborough, and about twelve miles from Easton, in Talbot County, Maryland." [xi]

"We are Americans, speaking the same language, adopting the same customs, holding the same general opinions... and shall rise and fall with Americans."

- Frederick Douglass

Chapter 4

African Migration

In 1660, the enslavement of Africans was legalized in Maryland and Virginia, USA. The Middle Passage was the journey between Africa and the Americas, which lasted two to three months. Africans were chained and crowded, with no space to move, and forced to endure the journey naked and lying in filth. Prior to the arrival of Portuguese trans-Atlantic slave traders, slavery and slave trading were already widespread throughout most of Africa. Enslavement was often a result of tribal rivalry, war, kidnapping, gambling, tribute, and criminal judgements. African slavery existed in various forms, ranging from mild forms of servitude to full-blown chattel slavery, commonly referred to as Islamic or market-based. Slavery in West Africa was seldom the harsh and pit less bondage as in the Americas."[xii] In the colonial era of Maryland, tobacco was the most valuable crop, used as a form of currency for trade. Tobacco had a significant impact on Maryland's economy and was a contributing factor in its development as a slave state."[xiii]

Oliver Downes's first known ancestor of African descent born in America was born sometime between the 1620s and 1790. By 1790, almost all Africans that were to be brought to America had already arrived. He or she only lived in Virginia and/or Maryland."[xiv] Ancestral African Americans had various statuses such as manumitted slaves, slaves-for-life, term slaves, or freeborn. Maryland's slavery system was different from the plantation type and was of the domestic type during the eighteenth century. Maryland did not have gradual emancipation laws like Pennsylvania, New York, and New Jersey, which ended slavery for life, and slaveholding was at the discretion of the slaveholders. "Approximately 90% of the slaveholders in the Eastern Shore had five or fewer enslaved individuals. Enslaved families lived near their White slaveholders."[xv]

In his book Narrative of the Life of Frederick Douglass, an American Slave, Frederick Douglass stated that "he had never met a slave who knew their own birthday, while White children were able to celebrate theirs. He was not allowed to inquire about it by his master and it was common in his part of Maryland to separate children from their mothers at a very young age. Often, before the child was even a year old, the mother was taken and hired out on a farm far away while the child was left under the care of an old woman who was too old to work in the fields. Douglass did not know why this was done, but believed it may have been to prevent the child from developing affection for their mother and to destroy the mother's natural affection for the child."[xvi] Frederick Douglass also stated, "that the men and women slaves received, as their monthly allowance of food, eight pounds of pork, or its equivalent in fish, and one bushel of corn meal. Their yearly clothing consisted of two coarse linen shirts, one pair of linen trousers, like the shirts, one jacket, one pair of trousers for winter, made of coarse cloth, one pair of stockings, and one pair of shoes; the whole of which could not have cost more than seven dollars. The allowance of the slave children was given to their mothers, or the old women having the care of them. The children unable to work in the field had neither shoes, stockings, jackets, nor trousers, given to them; their clothing consisted of two coarse linen shirts per year. When these failed them, they went naked until the next allowance-day. Children from seven to ten years old, of both sexes, almost naked, might be seen at all seasons of the year."[xvii]

DNA Cousins in Louisiana and Mississippi

Oliver Downes has DNA cousins from Louisiana and Mississippi who had no knowledge of their ancestors being from the Eastern Shore or had no familiar surnames. This could be explained by the wealthy slaveholders, such as the Lloyds, who bought cotton plantations in the South and moved their slaves from Maryland to Mississippi, Louisiana, and Arkansas. For instance, Edward Lloyd VI moved 200 slaves from his Maryland estate to start a new plantation in Madison County, Mississippi, in 1837."[xviii]

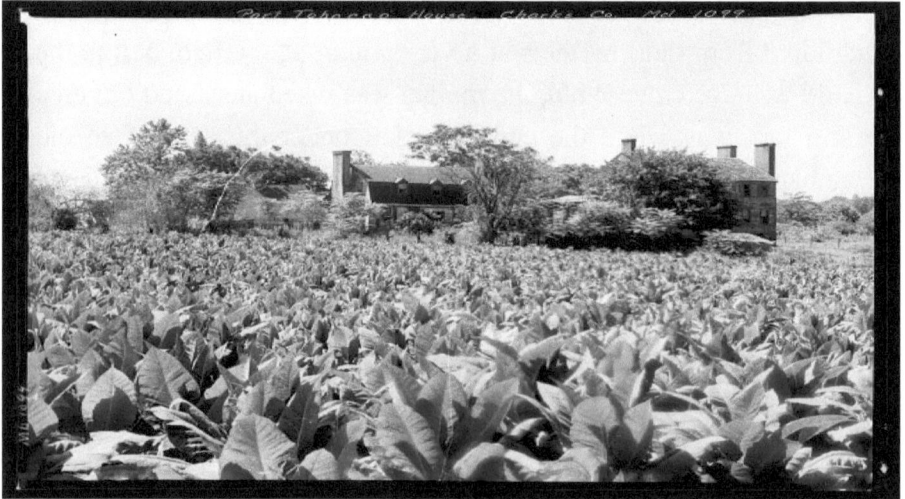

Figure 6. Port Tobacco Houses

Tool Notes: Typical sources of records that identify the enslaved persons would be owner records, journals, runaway slave advertisements, slave inventories, bibliographies of genealogies, bills of sale, and probate records (wills, inventories, distribution of estates, etc.) The Transatlantic Slave trade, 1527-1867 database. Local newspapers, Maryland Slave Narratives.

"I knew of blacks who were not slaves; I knew of whites who were not slaveholders; and I knew of persons who were nearly white, who were slaves. Color, therefore, was a very unsatisfactory basis for slavery."

- Frederick Douglass

Chapter 5

European Planters and the Indentures

The initial settlers in the Eastern Shore were tobacco and corn planters. The area was home to some of the most influential residents, including the Loockerman, Lloyds, Downes, Massey, Paca, Bordley, Tilghman, Sherwood, Jump, Green, Hardcastle, Wilson, Dashiel, Sparks, and Wooters families. Many of the earliest settlers in Maryland had their origins in the Jamestown settlement of English America. Large plantations were established as Lord Baltimore granted extensive lands to English immigrant families. During the first years of his Province of Maryland, 1633-1681, Lord Baltimore rewarded people who transported themselves or others with rights to land, usually called headrights. For most of the period, the reward was a right to fifty acres of land per person transported.[xix] To enter and exercise his rights, a person had to give the names of those, including himself, whom he had transported.[xx] The wealthy plantation owners were able to hire laborers, indentured servants, and convicts. As the supply of English servants became scarce, merchants turned to Scottish and Irish ports to recruit workers. From then on, half to two-thirds of all White immigrants to the American colonies were indentured servants for the next hundred years. The indentured servants were mostly employed as farm laborers and were bound to their masters for an average of four to six years. They were not paid cash wages, but instead were provided with food, housing, clothing, and training. It was also part of their contract not to marry or have children during the duration of their service.

Oliver's paternal great grandmother, Laura Downes nee Matthews, stated that her fore parents were of Canadian descent and were among the early settlers of Caroline County Maryland. "In 1755, four ships carrying over nine hundred Acadian exiles arrived in Maryland. Forcibly removed by the British from their homelands in Nova Scotia, Canada, these exiled Acadians were unceremoniously deposited on Maryland's shores and left to fend for themselves."[xxi] Is it possible that Laura Downes, previously known as Laura Matthews, had ancestors who came on one of the four ships? Scottish Jacobite prisoners of England were sold to men in Maryland.

"In the 18th century, around 50,000 convicts were sent from the British Isles to Colonial America, making up around one-fourth of all British immigrants. Their crimes ranged from minor offenses to murder. On the other hand, indentured immigrants who voluntarily committed for around seven years were typically of a more skilled and better background. However, despite their background, their indenture contract was typically for seven years, and they effectively became the property of the buyer." [xxii]

The Lloyds

"The Edward Lloyd Family became one of the largest slaveholders in Maryland."[xxiii]

"Edward Lloyd III was a plantation owner who owned multiple plantations on which he had enslaved over 150 men, women, and children. These plantations produced crops such as tobacco, corn, and wheat, and he also owned ships that traded with England, the West Indies, and New England. In addition, he rented out a portion of his land in Talbot and other Eastern Shore counties, as well as in Delaware. Lloyd was also involved in marketing his tobacco in

Britain and sold meat and livestock to butchers in Annapolis and Baltimore."[xxiv]

"During the American Revolution, the Wye Grist Mill, and hundreds of others like it on the Eastern Shore shipped barrels of flour via the Chesapeake Bay to the Continental Army, commanded by General George Washington. Historians dubbed the Eastern Shore the Breadbasket of the American Revolution."[xxv]

In Talbot County, in 1790, Edward Lloyd IV recognized that he owned 305 enslaved people, not including those on his properties in Dorchester and Queen Anne's counties.[xxvi] "Nearly all the plantations or farms in the vicinity of the 'home plantation' of Col. Lloyd, belong to him;and some people in the neighborhood of Col. Lloyd, such as the Skinners, the Peakers, the Tilghmans, the Lockermans, and the Gipsons, also own enslaved people and are just as committed to maintaining the system of slavery as Col. Lloyd. In fact, some of them are said to be even more strict than him, and their status as slaveholding neighbors may have reinforced their strict control over enslaved people."[xxvii]

The Skinners and Anthonys

Jenny, who was the great grandmother of Frederick Douglass, was born into slavery in 1746. She was owned by Richard Skinner, who was a tobacco planter in the Miles River Neck district of Talbot County in the Eastern Shore. It is possible that Bailey, an enslaved man born around 1701, was Jenny's father."[xxviii] "James and Esther Anthony lived in the Tuckahoe Neck area, which was a flat and marshy region east of Tuckahoe Creek in 1767. They were farmers who did not own any land or slaves and were considered poor. The area was part of Queen Anne's county at that time but was later incorporated into Caroline County. The region was populated by poor Whites and even poorer Black people, including slaves and free individuals who were known for their indolent and drunken behavior.."[xxix] Some years later, the Anthony's son Aaron Anthony resided in the Tuckahoe area of Queen Anne's County. Edward Lloyd IV hired Aaron Anthony as captain of his luxurious schooner, the Elizabeth & Ann. Edward Lloyd V provided rent free living quarters for the Aaron Anthony. Anthony married Anne Catherine Skinner, the daughter of Richard Skinner.

In 1797, James Anthony married Anne Catherine Skinner and became the owner of her slaves, whom he relocated to Holme Hill Farm in the Tuckahoe area of Talbot County. One of the slaves was Betsey Bailey, who was Frederick Douglass's grandmother, along with her daughters. Isaac Bailey, a free man of color, was hired by Aaron Anthony as a sawyer and lived near Holme Hill and Hillsboro, which was located close to Tuckahoe Creek. James Due, Oliver's fourth great-grandfather, was living nearby at the age of approximately forty-eight and working as a shoe cobbler. His first known son, Enoch Due, was living with him. On June 18, 1779, Virginia passed a bill declaring what persons shall be deemed mulattoes. "Be it enacted by the General Assembly, that every person, of whose grandfathers or grandmothers anyone is or shall have been, a negro, although all his other progenitors, except that descending from the negro, shall have been White persons, shall be deemed a mulatto, and so every person. Who shall have one fourth part or more of negro blood, shall be deemed a mulatto." [xxx] The one-drop Black blood is not in existence currently. After this time, Aaron Anthony was appointed as the chief administrator of the Lloyd agricultural operations, which included around thirteen farms and over ten thousand acres in Talbot County, as well as more than five hundred slaves. Anthony was responsible for taking care of the slaves and livestock, as well as managing business transactions. Later on, he purchased Holme Hill from his employer Edward Lloyd V, which included about two hundred acres of land, and it became the center of his real estate holdings in Talbot County.."[xxxi] Sometime after Isaac Bailey married Betsey Bailey and was the father of her eight children born after 1798. "Between 1799 and 1826, in addition to the ten children born to Betsey, her daughter

Milly had seven, Harriet at least six, Jenny three, Betty three, and Hester one."[xxxii]

It is probable that some of Oliver Downes's ancestors who lived in and around Hillsboro were enslaved by the Lloyds and may have intermarried with the Bailey family. Therefore, it is possible that Oliver could be related to Frederick Douglass through his uncles, aunts and cousins. Another possibility is through Frederick Douglass's older brother, Perry Downs, who claimed that his mother married a Downs and he was born after the marriage. Frederick Douglass's older brother, Perry Downes, stated, "My mother's name was Bailey, and she married a Downes; then I was born, then-then, well, I do not know who Fred's father was, but I have heard at one time he was the Governor of this here State of Maryland... That is all I know about it."[xxxiii] "There was a free Black man, Daniel Downs, living in Caroline County and rented property from Aaron Anthony."[xxxiv] Charles Downs and Benjamin Downs, who were both free Black individuals, also lived in the same area as Oliver Downes's ancestors. It is believed that these three families might have been related. There is a possibility that Benjamin Downs is the ancestor of Oliver Downes's lineage. Perry Downs suggested that the Governor of the State of Maryland or Edward Lloyd V could potentially be the father of Frederick Douglass.

The Downes

Henry Downes was born before 1640 in York River, Virginia and passed away in 1669 in Kent County, Maryland. His son, John Downes, was born around 1664 in British Colonial America's Virginia and worked as a carpenter. He married Margaret Hawkins in Queen Anne's, Maryland, around 1684, and had six sons and two daughters. John died at the age of 43 in approximately 1707 in Talbot, Maryland. Their children included Ann Downes, Charles Downes, John Hawkins Downes, James Downes, Margaret Downes, and Henry Downes. John's son, John Hawkins Downes, was born in

Talbot County in 1693 and died on May 6, 1756, in Queen Anne's County, Maryland. Edward Downes (1742-1796) was a plantation owner in Queen Anne's County.

John's grandson Philemon Downes (c.1741–c.1796) was sheriff of Queen Anne's County, Md., 1773–75, and served as the county's justice of the peace in 1778 and 1779. He moved to a farm in Caroline County in 1780 and was elected to the Maryland legislature in 1782 and 1795. John's niece, Henrietta Downes, married Thomas Hardcastle (ca. 1737-1808).

A Martha Downes manumitted her slave in 1796.

Document of Manumission: Pollodore and Martha Downes, Queen Anns County, Maryland, 1796 *State of Maryland Queen Anns County,*

Be it remembered that I Martha Downes of the county and state aforesaid, for divine good reasons and me thereunto moving do manumit and from bondage discharge my negro man called Pollodore, who being a slave was devised unto me as a legacy by my great late Grandfather Solomon Wright deceased and I do hereby declare the said Polladore to be fully and absolutely liberated and discharged from bondage forever and I do utterly disclaim all right of contract or interest in any and every kind of labor or service of the said Polladore from the day of the date hereof- And in testimony thereof I have set my hand and affixed my seal hereunto this fifth day of February, one thousand seven hundred and ninety six.

Martha Downes [xxxv]

"The Downes family set up themselves in the Ingleside area in the 1800s. There is a road near Ingleside, Ell Downes Road, which was named after their ancestor Eldridge Downes."[xxxvi] Oliver had noticed the Ell Downes Road sign on his way to visit his parents' house. One day, while driving by, he noticed the sign was lying on the ground. Oliver stopped the car, picked up the sign, and placed it in his car. When he returned home to West Chester, Pennsylvania, he placed the sign at the end of his driveway. The sign remained there for many years until someone eventually removed it.

The Bradleys

In 1729, Charles Bradley was residing in Tuckahoe Neck, Queen's County, and his family was influential in the county. They came from England in the latter part of the 17th century. John Bradley, the son of Nathaniel Bradley, inherited a plantation in Tuckahoe Neck and owned slaves, but freed them by 1810. Stephen J Bradley, born in Caroline County in 1808, was the son of John Bradley and Rebecca, daughter of Benjamin Jump. Stephen worked as a clerk in Captain Thomas Auld's store after leaving school in 1826. James Due, Oliver Downes' fourth great-grandfather, owned ten acres of land in the area that eventually became part of the Bradley farm. The land was inherited by John E. Starkey in 1856 from John Bradley, and James Due's parcel of land was among the seven inherited parcels, totaling approximately 960 acres in the vicinity of Bradleysburg/Hillsboro, Bridgetown, and Tuckahoe Creek in Caroline and Queen Anne's Counties. James Due was listed in the 1810 census with other Black men named Dan Hindsmen, Dan Downes, and Robert Rich, and his neighbor was John Bradley. Additionally, James Due reportedly received 50 acres of bounty land from the federal government for being a patriot but had to sell it to survive and retain the last ten acres.

The Jumps

In 1682 William Jump purchased land on the east side of Tuckahoe Creek, Furman's Grove, better known as Jumptown, which was one of the earliest settled portions of the county. When the county was formed, the Tuckahoe had been dammed and a mill near the present Crouse Mill was then in operation. Abraham Jump, also a prominent citizen in the county in his time. Josiah Jump was at one time clerk of the Circuit Court for Caroline County.

The Dues

Queens Anne County Judgement Records

In March 1751, John Dew, an orphan son of John Dew, bound to Caleb Escate. William Dew, an orphan of John Dew, bound to Thomas Sands. August 1751, James Dew, orphan son of John, bound to Philemon Thomas to age 21, being four years in November next. November 1751, Mary Dew, an orphan of John Dew, bound to Joseph Elliot. [xxxvii] Could this be Oliver's 4th great-grandfather James Due and his siblings? This James was born about 1748. In great-grandfather's James Due pension records, he said he was born about 1758. Do not get too hung up on fluctuating birth dates, because people before the 20th century paid little attention to their birthdays and routinely did not keep an account of their birth year. Oliver's James did sign up for the war in Queens Anne County.

In 1777 or 1778 John Due signed the Maryland Oaths of Fidelity in Queen Anne's County. I did not see a James Due's name on the list. [xxxviii]

"The whisper that my master was my father, may or may not be true; and, true or false, it is of but little consequence to my purpose whilst the fact remains."

- Frederick Douglass

Narrative of the Life of Frederick Douglass: An American Slave, (1841)

.

Chapter 6

Multiracial People "New People" of the America

Oliver Downes Sr., Edwina, Rosalie, and Vella underwent DNA testing, which revealed that they have a significant amount of European DNA. Specifically, Oliver Sr. has 29%, Edwina has 31%, Rosalie has 27%, and Vella has 29% European DNA. Additionally, Oliver's niece, Avis Schwartz, inherited 14% European DNA from her mother, Ellen. Despite having no known White ancestors from his parents to his great-grandparents, Oliver and his siblings' skin complexion ranged from brown to beige, and most of them had hazel eyes, which suggests a long history of interracial mixing during the colonial era. The first generation of multiracial slave children were called African Creoles, by the citizens of the English America. African Creoles were descendants of African women and Portuguese men who worked at the slave ports and on the boats. Barbados was the first English colony to develop a significant mixed-heritage population, followed by Jamaica and the provinces of Virginia and Maryland- where the highest levels of ethnoracial mixing occurred between Africans and Europeans in colonial North America.[xxxix] It is believed that many children of enslaved people from the second and third generations may have had White fathers who were slaveholders, slave drivers, family members, guests, or overseers, but it is not the only possibility.

"British courts during the first century of settlement sentenced some 4,400 criminals, paupers, and other undesirables to servitude in the Chesapeake colonies. It seems highly probable that these White servants, voluntarily and involuntarily, contributed much to the foundation of a large mulatto population in the American colonies."[xl] Oliver and his siblings have DNA matches with White individuals who share surnames common to the Eastern Shore Maryland such as Ayres, Cooper, Deshields, Dhue, DuHadaway, Flamer, Stanley, and Wyatt. "By an act of 1681, children born of White women and Black men, were free. After 1692, the issue of a union between any White woman with a slave or free Black, became servants for a long time. During the colonial period in Maryland and Delaware: Over 600 free, mixed-race children were born to White women by Black men. As in other colonies, both enslaved and free Black people intermarried with European indentured. Also Blacks and Whites intermarried with Native Americans."[xli] A law enacted in 1715 forbade, under penalties, the marriage of a White to any Black person or multiracial slave. But by this law a White and a free multiracial person could marry.

Below are excerpts from *Free African Americans of Maryland and Delaware from the Colonial Period to 1810* by Paul Heinegg[xlii] that might pertain to Oliver Downes ancestors that might had White progenitors.

Downes

Eliza Downes, born around 1708, was the servant of Sarah Dashiell of Stepney Parish, and on 15 March 1725/6 the Somerset County court ordered that she be sold for seven years for having an illegitimate child [Judicial Record 1725-7, 97]. She may have been the ancestor of Charles, "Negro" head of a Caroline County household of 7 "other free" in 1810.

Ben, "Negro" head of a Caroline County household of 7 "other free" in 1810.

Daniel, "Negro" head of a Caroline County household of 5 "other free" in 1810.

Pritchett

1. Ann Pritchard, born say 1748, was a spinster living in Queen Anne's County on 10 May 1767, when she had an illegitimate "Molatto" child by a "Negro man." The court ordered that she be sold for seven years after she completed her service to James Sudler [Judgment Records 1766-7, part 1, CD image 100]. She was probably the mother of the five-year-old "Mulatto" girl serving until the age of twenty-one when she was listed in the Queen Anne's County inventory of James Sudler on 8 April 1773 [Prerogative Inventories 113:199]. She may have been the ancestor of James, head of a Talbot County household of 3 "other free" in 1800 [MD:531].

Another member of a Prichard/ Pritchett family was Silas Pritchett, manumitted by Solomon Barwell in Kent County, Delaware, on 20 October, 1786 [Delaware Archives RG 3555.55], head of a Kent County, Maryland household of 5 "other free" in 1800 [MD:63].

Flamer

John was born say 1717, a "Molatto" servant man having "eleven months and 15" to serve and valued at 4 pounds in the inventory of the Queen Anne's County estate of William Hernsley, on 28 October, 1737 [Prerogative Inventories 1737-1739, 45-6]. He had an illegitimate child by Elizabeth Grinnage in September 1736 [Judgment Record 1735-9, 344, 382]. He may have been identical to Jonathan Flamar, who owed 994 pounds to the Queen Anne's County estate of Solomon Clayton (who died in 1739) [Prerogative Inventories 98:18-22].

ii. William, was born say 1717, a "Molatto" servant man having "eleven months and 15" to serve and valued at 4 pounds in the inventory of the Queen Anne's County estate of William Hernsley, on 28 October, 1737 [Prerogative Inventories 1737-1739, 45-6].

1. Rachel Flamer, born say 1720, a "poor old woman," was supported from public funds by the Queen Anne's County from 12 December, 1775, to 1787. She was called a "poor molatto woman" by the court when it approved her allowance for 1777 [Surles, and they appeared at Court, 1774-1777, 65, 80; 1779, 1782, 1785, 1786, 1787, 35, 53, 89, 96, 117]. She may have been the ancestor of

2. Judith Flamer, was born say 1722, was the servant (no race indicated) of Mark Hargadine of Saint Paul's Parish in March, 1745, when the Queen Anne's County court convicted her of having an illegitimate child named John in 1742, and another child in 1743. In August 1750, she confessed to having other children on 10 June ,1747, and 10 December, 1748 [Judgment Record 1744-6, 161-2; 1750, 40-2]. She was a spinster living in St. Paul's Parish when she received thirty lashes and was ordered to pay four-fold the value for stealing a hog worth forty pounds [Criminal Record 1751-9, n.p.]. She owed the estate of Thomas Kendall four pounds, nineteen shillings on 10 August, 1756 [Prerogative Inventories 73:243]. She was the mother of

i. John 2, born on 10 October, 1742, a "black" taxable in the Upper Hundreds of Kent Island, Queen Anne's County in 1776 [Carothers, 1776 Census of Maryland, 148], married to Sherry Grinnage's daughter Sarah on 1 November, 1790, when Sherry gave her 5 pounds currency by his Caroline County will [WB JR B:168-70].

ii. Ann, mother of William and John Flamer (no race indicated) who were with George Sweat on 26 January 1774 when the Queen Anne's County court ordered him to bring them to court [Surles, and they Appeared at Court, 1774-1777, 41], perhaps identical to the "Molatto girl named Nan" who was valued at 16 pounds in the inventory of the Queen Anne's County estate of William Hernsley on 28 October 1737 [Prerogative Inventories 1737-1739, 45-6].

iii. Solomon, head of a Queen Anne's County household of 9 "other free" in 1790 [MD:99] and 9 in 1800 [MD:341].

iv. William, head of a Talbot County household of 1 "other free" and three slaves in 1800 [MD:506].

From the book *Praise the Bridge that Carries You Over the Life of Joseph Sutton* by Shepard Krech III, "Joseph Sutton said that his grandmother, Charlotte, married Alex Flamer. He was my mother's father. The Flamers were free. My grandfather Flamer's mother had not heard nothin' about when they were set free, they had the whole generation of that day come up as free people and that was unusual, and then the Flamers bought little farms and things were the slaves was not able to buy 'em, because they had gotten the start on 'em. My grandfather, Flamer, had a brother. He owns two farms. What they called the 'Big Farm' was in Talbot. It was right on the line and that is where all the Flamers was, some over the line in Talbot and some over on the Queen Anne side."[xliii]

The Johns

In 1822, Margaret Johns, a twenty-eight-year-old mulatto, the daughter of Ann Ayers, a White woman, and Hercules Johns, a slave, applied for a freedom certificate before the Talbot County Clerk. A witness testified to the clerk that since infancy Margaret had lived freely in Easton with her White mother, who, "during all the time this deponent knew her, cohabited with a Negro man slave named Hercules who called himself Hercules Johns."[xliv]

"Europe and Africa are already here, and the Indian was here before either."

- **Frederick Douglass**

1887 speech called "Our Composite Nation"

.

Chapter 7

Native Americans

Oliver and his sisters did not have detectable Indigenous American DNA, but that does not necessarily mean they lacked Indigenous American ancestry. It is possible that they did not inherit that DNA or that their Indigenous American ancestors were too distant to be detected by the test. However, it is still possible that other siblings might have measurable Indigenous American DNA. Based on historical records, it is believed that their Indigenous American ancestors originated from the Powhattan Confederacy. The Powhatan Confederacy was a political, social, and martial entity of over 30 Algonquian-speaking Native American tribes of the region of modern-day Virginia, Maryland, and part of North Carolina, USA.[xlv]

On the Eastern Shore, there were five main tribes: the Choptank, Susquehannocks, Lenape (also known as the Delaware), Matapeake, and Nanticoke. These tribes followed a matriarchal society. While researching Samuel Pritchett, I came across Mitsawokett, a website that provided information on a Native American community from the 17th century. According to this website, Samuel Pritchett's lineage had connections with the Lenape and Nanticoke tribes. I am grateful for the assistance provided by Cousins John C. Carter, the late Betty Davis Terry, Ray Terry, and others who gathered the valuable data for this website.[xlvi]

When I searched for information on Ruffin Acree, who was Oliver's maternal second great-grandfather, in 2012, I came across an older post on the Acree Family Genealogy forum. The post was dated from an earlier time.

"December 25, 1998,
Merry Christmas greetings from Canada.
I am doing Powhatan genealogy, and I am looking for ancestors/descendants of Ruffin Acree (b. 1821) of King and Queen County, Virginia, and his wife, Peggy Ann (b. 1830).
They had one son, Leroy/Lee (b. 1861 – d. 1910) who had two marriages, both with women named Byrd. I see a lot of Acrees today named Cathy Lee and Deborah Lee, etc., which curiously indicates some affinity for "Lee" among the Acrees. Any information you have will be gladly received and reciprocated. Best regards.
Rarihokwats"[xlvii]

In 2012, I was thrilled to have found evidence confirming what my grandmother, Mary Grace Acree, had told me about her father, William Oliver, being of Native American heritage. William Oliver Acree was the grandson of Ruffin Acree and Peggy Ann Fortune, and the nephew of Lee Acree. However, I felt ashamed for not listening attentively to my grandmother when she first shared this information with me. At that time, I was not prepared to accept it.

Despite my doubts, I decided to reach out to Rarihokwats, whose email address I had found on a post from 1998. Rarihokwats is the historian and genealogist for the Powhatan nation. To my surprise, he responded to my email. Rarihokwats informed me that two of Lee and Nora (Byrd) Acree's descendants are currently members of the Powhatan Renape Nation. However, Lee's family has not been linked to the known Acree members of the Pamunkey and Mattaponi communities. However, Lee's acceptance into the household of

James Byrd, a known Rappahannock, his marriage to two Byrd women, and the fact that two of his siblings also married a Byrd is indicative that Lee was "Indian" and was related to the known Indian Acree families. Rarihokwats was not aware, but I discovered that Ruffin Acree's wife, Peggy Ann, was Peggy Ann Fortune. It is worth noting that Caroline County Virginia was a significant hub for the Rappahannock people. Rarihokwats was conducting research with Chief Roy Crazy Horse on Native American information in the Caroline County Virginia courthouse. During their investigation, Rarihokwats also researched genealogy related to the Nanticoke and Delaware tribes, as there were planned marriages between the Morristown community.

The Powhatan center in New Jersey and the Maryland/Delaware Nanticoke tribe aimed to bring in new members to prevent excessive intermarriage. Rarihokwats explained that the Powhatan Renape Nation genealogy has two primary roots, and two secondary roots, all four leading to state recognized tribes. The two primary roots are the Rappahannock Tribe of Virginia, and the Nanticoke Tribe of Delaware. The two secondary roots go to the Chickahominy and Mattaponi/Pamunkey Tribes of Virginia. There was a high percentage of intermarriage within the same four Indigenous communities until and after the time when the Powhatan Renape Nation had grown to a sufficient size to allow intermarriage within its own membership. I asked Rarihokwats if he had any information on Samuel Pritchett, Oliver's third great-grandfather, but he replied that he did not. However, he did note that the Delaware Pritchetts had married into the Mosley and Carney families, both of which were Powhatan Renape names in New Jersey. Rarihokwats explained that the racial identity issues in the Powhatan community arose due to their persecution, which prompted them to adopt a survival strategy of integrating with free Black communities. While intermarriage did occur, the Powhatan community also practiced homemade genetics to maintain the Powhatan bloodline. Children were taught to "marry right," which meant to marry partners who most closely resembled Powhatans in terms of appearance. The Fortunes, of course, have been active in the Rappahannock Nation in Virginia. Their neighbors were Parkers, Nelsons, and Byrd, and Tazewell Fortune's parents lived next door to Chief Roy Crazy Horse's ancestors, Daniel, and Simon Johnson, and on the other side of the Johnsons lived Mordecai Byrd. Rappahannock names are remarkably familiar to all to Chief Roy Crazy Horse: the Rollins, the Byrds, Johnson, Nelson, and of course, Acree. Oliver Downes can trace his family roots back to both the Fortunes and Acrees. Ruffin Acree was the offspring of Major Acree and Nancy Carter, and he was born in approximately 1826, in King and Queen County, Virginia. He wed Peggy Ann Fortune, who was also born in King and Queen County, Virginia around 1831. Together, they had a son named Robert Acree, who was born in King and Queen County, Virginia, in 1848. Robert Acree eventually relocated to Maryland, where he married Mary Johns. Robert Acree is Oliver's great-grandfather and is the progenitor of the Eastern Shore Acrees of color.

"Heaven's blessing must attend all, and freedom must soon be given to the pining millions under a ruthless bondage."

\- **Frederick Douglass**

My Bondage and My Freedom

Chapter 8

Free person of color: An ambiguous designation that may include individuals of undetermined quantities of African, Native American, and European ancestry. Often refers to non-white without showing racial identity.[xlviii]

Maryland Quakers came out against slavery, and then the Methodist Conference, in 1780, declared that slavery was "contrary to laws of God, man, and nature, and hurtful to society."[xlix] By the 1800s, most free African Americans in Maryland had bought their freedom through manumission.

Most of Oliver Downes's ancestors who were people of color were freed by 1830, although it is unclear when exactly this happened in their family lineages. It is known that free Black people have been living in Maryland and Virginia since the 1600s. In 1665, Anthony Johnson, a Black Angolan farmer from Virginia, and his family sold their 250-acre land and relocated to Somerset County, Maryland, where they leased a 300-acre land. Anthony Johnson has been recognized as "the Black patriarch" of the initial community of Black property owners in America."[l] The Hill Community in Easton was established by free Black individuals in Talbot County in 1788. They purchased properties, founded two African American churches, and worked for locals in the area. Maryland enacted a law in 1790 that permitted slaveholders to free their slaves through wills or deeds, making manumissions the first legal agreements between a free person and a formerly enslaved individual that were recognized by the state."[li]

"By 1800, the area's free Black population hit an all-time high. More than a third of Dorchester County's African American population, for instance, was free. Part of this had to do with region's high number of Quakers, who started freeing their slaves long before the Civil War ended and went on to be agents of the Underground Railroad." [lii] Oliver's ancestors could have adopted their last name from a former slaveholder or a slaveholder of a prior generation in their family line. Enslaved individuals often took on the name of a previous owner as a means of reclaiming their history and creating a connection to their ancestral family.

List of known surnames in Oliver Downes's tree living in the Eastern Shore Maryland:

Acree	Downes	Johns	Sparks
Cephas	Due/Dhue	Lockerman	Talbot
Clark	Flamer	Matthews	Turner
Cooper	Homer	Pritchett	Wyatt

The number of free individuals of color in Maryland and other states was on the rise, but the White inhabitants believed that they had a negative impact on the enslaved population. To address this issue, the American Colonization Society was established in the U.S. House of Representatives in Washington, DC, with the goal of relocating free persons of color outside the United States. Some of the group's founding members were southern political leaders and slave owners, such as Henry Clay, John C. Calhoun, Bushnell Washington, and Francis Scott Key. The society was exclusive to White members and did not oppose slavery either legally or morally. In 1831, the Maryland General Assembly approved a law with the aim of relocating free African Americans out of the state of Maryland to support the Maryland State Colonization Society's effort to transport them to West Africa and the Caribbean.

Oliver has a DNA relative who has a Sub-Saharan heritage of 99% and came from Monigo, Liberia. This relative's grandparents are named Deans and Merchants. She mentioned that her ancestors on her mother's side migrated to the United States and were among the freed slaves who returned to Africa when President Monroe authorized it. Her family, along with many others, helped establish Liberia. In Liberia, a region called the Republic of Maryland was established by freed African American slaves and freeborn African Americans, mainly from Maryland, USA, in 1834 under the guidance of the Maryland State Colonization Society.[liii]

The Maryland General Act was to record the free people of color in 1832. The county sheriffs recorded the names, sexes, and ages of all the free African Americans within their jurisdiction, including those living in White households. This census took place a full 31 years before the Emancipation Proclamation.

Free African-Americans of Maryland 1832 abstracted by Jerry M. Hynson[liv]

Below is partial list of free Negroes in Caroline County Presented By Robert T. Kune, Sheriff in a probable family unit that I thought was significant to Oliver Downes's lineages of known names.

Moses Coker, 60. Grace Coker, 45. Isaac Coker, 22. Moses Coker Jr., 20.

Henry Coker, 21. Catherine Coker, 15. Susan Coker, 13. Ellen Coker, 9.

Henry Cooper, 15 Robert Cooper, 27 George Cooper Charlotte Cooper, 10 John Cooper William Cooper Charles Cooper.
Joseph Matthews, 44. Ann Hawkins, 100. Henry Matthews, 25. Henry Miller, 22. Ann Matthews, 17. John Matthews, 13. Henrietta Matthews, 11. Benedict Matthews, 9. William Matthews, 6.

Anderson Matthews, 2. James Matthews, 1. Mary Matthews, 3 months.

Benjamin Downs, 60. Margaret Downs, 45.

Benedict Wyatt, 27. Clementine Wyatt Nathaniel Elizabeth Wyatt, 35. James Wyatt, 35. Nancy Wyatt, 65. William Wyatt, 35. Elizabeth Wyatt, 14. James Wyatt, 12. Mary Wyatt, 10. Caroline Wyatt, 8. William Wyatt, 6. ____Wyatt, 3. John Wyatt, 6 months.

Isaac Downs, 22. Harriet Downs, 33. Isaac Downs, 32. Harris A. Downs, 33. John Williams, 60. Henry Williams, 55. Margaret___, 18. Montgomery Downs, 9. William Downs, 5. Elizabeth Downs, 2.

John Wyatt, 41. Maria Wyatt, 43. Samuel Wyatt, 19. Ellen Wyatt, 17. John Wyatt Jr., 15. Henry Wyatt, 13.Maria Wyatt, 11. Adeline Wyatt, 8. Sarah Wyatt, 6. Charles Wyatt, 1.

John Lockerman, 27. Sarah Lockerman, 27. Elizabeth A. Lockerman, 21. Rebecca Lockerman, 2.

Daniel Downs, 60. Diana Downs, 64.

David Lockerman, 40. Allen Murray, 52. Lydia Murray, 45. Catherine Murray, 20. Mary Murray, 15. Emily Murray, 10. Rhonda Murray, 9. Richard B. Murray Harriet Hemsley, 4. John W. Lockerman, 3.

Benjamin Downs, 30. Sarah Downs, 30. Francis Wayman, 49. Mathilda Wayman, 45. John Wayman, 18. Joseph Wayman, 15. Alexander Wayman, 12. Benjamin Wayman, 9. William H. Wayman, 5. Robert Francis Wayman, 2.

Henry Stanford, 47. Nancy Stanford, 40. Thomas Stanford, 11. Lydia Stanford, 6. John H. Stanford, 5. Stephen Stanford, 4. Susan Stanford, 70. Thomas Stanford, 60.

Charles Downs, 45. Rachel Hooper, 33. William Downs, 19. E Downs, 16. Charles Downs, 10. Downs, 6. Susan Downs, 8. Henry Downs, 4.Nancy Downs John Downs, 20.

L Johns, 49. DJohns, 23. Mary Jane Johns, 22. Matthew U. Johns, 19. Henry L. Johns, 18. Hannah H. Johns, 14. N_Jefferson Johns, 12. Eliza Ann Johns, 10. Catherine A. Johns, 8. Alexander Johns, 5. William F, 3. Asbury F Johns, 8 months.

Ann Cephas, 15. Harrison Cephas, 30. Sarah Cephas, 20. Daniel Cephas, 5 months.

Partial Listing of Free Negroes in Dorchester County

Henry Cephas, 15. Joseph Cephas, 80. Emory Dobson, 10. Charles Dobson, 30. Josiah Cephas, 6. Moses Stanley, 3. John Cephas, 13. Moses Cephas, 75.

Matthew Johns, 2. Jacob Cephas, 50. Henry Johns, 11. Josiah Cephas, 10. Bill Johns, 19. John Cephas, 4. Bob Johns, 23. Thomas Cooper, 56.

Dick Cephas, 20. John Cephas, 19. Joe Cephas, 14. Levin Cephas, 12. Sam Cephas, 70. Howan Matthews, 11. Ann Johns, 1. Betsy A. Cephus, 2.

Ann Johns, 12. Prissy Ross, 60. Mary Cephus, 25. Nicy Cooper, 22. John Cooper, 9. Eliza Cephus, 7. Ralph Tubman, 51. Rachel Cephus, 6.

Thomas Cooper, 12. Rachel Cephus, 55. John Cooper, 10. Harriet Cephus, 19. William Cooper, 8. Henry Cephus, 12. Samuel Cooper, 1. Tubman Tubman, 10.

Fanny Cephus, 70. Joshua Lockerman, 50. Rosy Stanley, 16. Mary Stanley, 18.

Sophia Cephus, 40. Thomas Lockerman, 20. Ritty Cephus, 12. George Lockerman, 18.

Eliza Stanley, 4. Caroline Cephus, 15. Sophia Cephus, 7. David Lockerman, 1.

Lina Cephus, 50. Robert Lockerman, 8. Mary Cephus, 27. Eliza A. Cephus, 9.

Charlotte Stanley, 30. John C Tubman, 15. Sarah Cooper, 56. Henry Ross, 55.

Mary Cooper, 16. John Tubman, 38. Mary Ross, 33. Rachel Cephus, 50.

Ann Ross, 20. Deborah Johns, 37. Martha Cephus, 70. Mary Johns, 25.

Jinny Cephus, 23. Matilda Cephus, 13. Mary J. Cephus, 10. Nancy Matthews, 45.

Partial Listing of Free People of Color Residing in Queen Anne's County.

Thomas Pritchett, 13. Joseph Ayres, 13. Benjamin Duhamel, 7. Elizabeth Downes, 35.

Edward Downes, 60. Luther Ayres, 8. John Duhamel, 2. Rose Bailey, 60.

Jerry Dobson, 14. William Pritchett, 24. George Ayres, 60. Hannah Bailey, 40.

Harry Ayres, 40. Thomas Pritchett, 16. Luther Ayres, 6. Ellen Downes, 5.

Henry Dobson, 4. Samuel Pritchett, 10. Levi Downes, 5. Maria Downes, 32.

James Dobson, 2. William H. Pritchett, 1. Charles H. Downes, 1. Sarah Downes, 8.

Stephen Downes, 31 Philip Pritchett, 4 Samuel Rochester, 4 Richard Rochester, 59

Benjamin Downes, 3 Oyster Pritchett, 1 Abraham Rochester, 65 Daphny Downes, 70

William Downes, 9 Joseph Lockerman, 55 Oneal Comegys, 35 Hannah Pritchett, 46

Henry Comegys, 3 William Lockerman, 7 Lewis Comegy, 75 Sally Pritchett, 21

George Ayres, 32 Cornelious Comegys, 50 Jacob Downes, 45 Hannah A. Pritchett,

Arthur Ayres, 32. Samuel Comegys, 6. Sherry Flamer, 30. Memory Bordley, 35.

Joseph Dobson, 55. Jacob Duhamel, 62. Nicholas Flamer, 15. Henny Bordley.

Charles Ayres, 6. William H. Duhamel, 15. Arthur Rochester, 25. Henrietta Bordley, 7.

Mary Pritchett, 15. Ann Pritchett, 15. Jenny Lockerman, 50.

Partial Listing of Free Blacks Residing in Talbot County 1832.[lv]

Emanuel Downes, 34. Benjamin Lockerman, 25. Benjamin Pritchett, 41. Charlotte Downes, 28.

Eliza Lockerman, 24. Ann Pritchett, 39. Matilda Ann Gross, 12. Elizabeth Loockerman, 6.

Juda Pritchett, 54. Henrietta Gross, 10. John Lockerman, 7. James Pritchett, 14.

Martha Ann Gross, 2. Ann Pritchett, 12. George Downes, 7. Hector Downes, 50.

Henry Pritchett, 9. Sarah Downes, 40. Thomas Pritchett, 2. Sarah Barrett, 40.
Catherine Downes, 14. Martha Gross, 45. Martha Ann Downes, 15. Edward Downes, 31.

Charles Barrett, 8. Susan Downes, 12. Sophiah Downes, 28. David Gross, 14.

James Bennett, 13. Rachel Bordley, 83. John Johns, 45. Zarah Downes, 32.

Darcus Downes, 33. Eliza Downes, 18. William Downes, 5. Emaline Sherwood, 27.

Thomas Downes, 3. John Downes, 3. Emily Downes, 8. Juby Downes, 60.

Roderic Downes, 45. Caty Stanton, 90. Frisby Nichols, 24. Joseph Cephus, 70.

Jeremiah Matthews, 40. Ruth Ann Downes, 45. Margaret Matthews, 50. John Anderson, 5.

Elizabeth Downes, 12. Susan Matthews, 15. Eliza Matthews, 12. Hannah Dolphin, 60.

John Turner, 19. Solomon Flamer, 3. George Flamer, 9. Lucy Flamer, 20.

John Flamer, 70. Caroline Flamer, 7. Mary Paca, 12. Charity Flamer, 50.

Maria Flamer, 4. Sidney Flamer, 35. Daniel King, 60. Martha Flamer, 4.

Charity Flamer, 19. Cata King, 50. Nancy Flamer, 16. Harriet King, 20.

Airy Flamer, 55. Nancy Ann Flamer, 9. Matilda Johns, 35. Nancy Flamer, 18.

James Flamer, 4. Stevens John, 5. Martha Ann Jones, 2. Mary Cooper, 25.

Julia Cephus, 35. Mary Johns, 2. Edward Cooper, 2. Elsbury Armstrong, 13.

Henry King, 1. Martha Armstrong, 11. Ennals Stewart, 20.

Tool Kit: Starting from the 1790 federal census, records show that Free African Americans were present in the United States. To regulate the issuance of freedom papers, the General Assembly created a law that aimed to identify such individuals. The law mandated African Americans who were born free to provide proof of their freedom to the county court. The court then issued a certificate of freedom after verification of the documents. In cases where the Black person had been freed from slavery, the court clerk or register of wills would verify the manumitting document before issuing a certificate of freedom. Besides information on how the individual obtained freedom, the certificate also included physical characteristics, such as height, eye color, complexion, and hair texture, which could be used for identification purposes.

"I make no pretension to patriotism. So long as my voice can be heard on this or the other side of the Atlantic, I will hold up America to the lightning scorn of moral indignation. In doing this, I shall feel myself discharging the duty of a true patriot; for he is a lover of his country who rebukes and does not excuse its sins. It is righteousness that exalteth a nation while sin is a reproach to any people."

- Frederick Douglass

Speech, "Love of God, Love of Man, Love of Country", Syracuse, New York (September 24, 1847).

Chapter 9

How I Found the Patriot James Due

James Due is the oldest verified direct ancestor linking him to Oliver Downes Sr., who is his fourth great-grandfather. While conducting research on Ancestry.com in August 2017, it was discovered that a family tree had been created containing information about Serena, Oliver's third great-grandmother who was married to Samuel Pritchett. What made this entry interesting was that the owner of the tree had listed Serena's maiden name was Due, which was previously unknown. After confirming that the owner of the tree was a DNA-tested cousin, I contacted them to ask how they had arrived at the conclusion that Serena's maiden name was Due. The following correspondence contains their response.

Sep 06, 2017

Hi Stephani, nice to meet you. I see the DNA match with your father on ancestry.com. The match is with my father. After looking at our shared DNA matches, I agree that we appear to be cousins through the Dhue line, with a common ancestor of James Dew/Due/Dhue. James was the father of Serena (your ancestor) and Enoch (my ancestor). Since both Serena and Enoch were born out of wedlock to an unknown mother, they could be full siblings or half siblings. Either way James Dhue is their father. This line is very interesting because there is either American Indian or African heritage in the Dhues. I only found that out after getting into genealogy research because the census records show fluctuating data in the race field. I wish I could tell you that I have a ton of information on the Dhues, but they have been a tough family to research, and I have some dead ends as well. My dad's information on them is very limited. I do feel confident about the line back to James Dhue though. Thank goodness James had a war pension record and real estate in Caroline County that helped confirm his children's names. One thing that we could do to completely understand the DNA match is to see what strand we match on. Then others that we find with that strand would also be descended from James Dhue. Since ancestry.com does not have a chromosome browser, we would need to do that comparison on gedmatch.com or ftdna.com (family tree DNA), both of which are free and both of which I have uploaded my dad's DNA to. Let me know if you think that would be a good idea. Overall, it looks like James Dhue passed on DNA to us on chromosomes 10 and 15, and that DNA managed to survive through the years.

Joanna

Joanna's assistance didn't end with providing Serena's maiden name. She went above and beyond by sending me several documents that established the relationship between James Due and his children. I searched for the name "Dhue" on Ancestry.com's DNA search section and found that Oliver shares DNA with multiple individuals who are descendants of James Dhue/Due. This provides conclusive evidence that Oliver is indeed a descendant of James Due. I also reached out to another DNA-tested cousin named Leslie, who was also helpful. Although Leslie is also a descendant of Enoch Dhue, it was through a different child than Joanna's. Below is a letter from Leslie.

Oct 16, 2017

I was just searching the Maryland state archives online and I found were James Due recognized his children as his own but because of the laws, that since they were born out of wedlock and owned by him; they could not be his heirs. Here is the link.

http://msa.maryland.gov/megafile/msa/speccol/sc2900/sc2908/000001/000213/html/am213--228.html

Once I get to my laptop, I will link the document to the correct people.

Leslie

My Letter to Leslie

Oct 16, 2017

Now it appears that James Due, had a concubine of color and he claimed the children from this union. Now she could have been African, or Native American, or Mulatto (African and European). I personally think she was all three. The children were fair in complexion, that eventually Enoch chose to live as White, which I do not consider passing, but that is another story. James's children were free, meaning their mother was free at the time of births. I do not know how Enoch's brother John and sister Rachel chose to live their life. But this not unusual for me, I have several family lineages of Maryland and Virginia, where I have seen the siblings chose different paths, unfortunately their descendants do not want to correspond. People do not want to know how they got the tiny piece of Sub-Saharan African dot on their graph or could get completely washed out. Folks do not want to know that especially in the North, there were miscegenation relationships, which did not involve rapes in the 1700s. The White indenture servants did have relationships with free people of color or the enslaved. The Native Americans did have relationship with the Europeans and the Africans. So, since James had four children, who legally should not have his inheritance, he made a point to put them in his will, unfortunately he did not mention their mother's name.

Stephani

Joanna and Leslie, who are Caucasian descendants of Serena Due's brother Enoch, also known as Dhue, along with other DNA-tested cousins who are descendants of James Due, have suggested the possibility of Native American or African heritage in the Dhue family line. Leslie also expressed a belief that James Due or the mother of his children might have been Native American. This finding may support the family's oral history of Native American ancestry in Oliver's lineage, which was a significant breakthrough for the family's Pritchett lineage research. The author notified several other cousins, including Gerald Scott, Dean Henry, Yolanda Acree, Edward Harris, Brenda Harris, and Terry Brown, who were also researching the Pritchett lineage and struggling with finding information about Samuel and Serena Pritchett. I shared with them the news that Serena Pritchett's family had been found and that her father was a soldier in the American Revolutionary War. Additionally, I discovered direct descendants of Enoch Dhue still living on the Eastern Shore, Noble Dhue, and his nephew, Andrew Dhue, who provided valuable information about their family's lineage and expressed excitement about meeting their cousin from their great aunt Serena Due-Pritchett when the author returns to the Eastern Shore.

James Due

James Due served in the Continental Army for nine months in Queen Anne's County and then re-enlisted for three years under Captain Hawkins in the 5th Maryland regiment. He was captured at Elizabethtown and was released after ten months, after which he fought in the Battle of Yorktown. He was discharged on November 15, 1783, in Annapolis, Maryland. However, while reviewing his information on Ancestry.com, it was discovered that in the 1810 United States Federal Census, James Due and Daniel Downes were both listed as Negro Men in Caroline County, Maryland, which was surprising since it was previously assumed that James Due was White and the mother of his children was either Black, Native American, or multiracial. In the 1820 United States Federal Census, James Due was listed as a free man of color. It was found that James was indeed a free man of color and was listed as such in the resource called *Forgotten Patriots: African American and American Indian Service in the Revolutionary War, 1775-1783*, where he was listed as "Due/Dice, James, African American ('Negro'), Private, S34711" in the Maryland chapter. "[lvi]

As a researcher, I had made an incorrect assumption that James Due, the 4th great-grandfather of Oliver Downes Sr., was a White patriot while the mother of Serena was of African descent. However, it turns out that James Due was an African American patriot of the American Revolution, and his children included Enoch, Rachel, John, and Serena. There was a lack of racial descriptions in most records of patriots during that period, although some sources may refer to them as "Negro," "Black," "mulatto," or "Indian." Enoch, who was born around 1792 in Caroline County, Maryland and died on October 22, 1884, in Greensboro, Caroline County, Maryland, went by the spelling of Dhue, as did his descendants. Rachel Due was born around 1804 in Caroline County, Maryland, while John Due was born around the same time in the same place. Finally, Serena, Oliver's 3rd great-grandmother, was born in Caroline

County, Maryland, in 1810. The following pages contain documents that provide information about James Due and his children.

Military and Pension Fact:

Southern Campaigns Revolutionary War Pension Statement

("S34771 James Due - revwarapps.org")

Originally transcribed and annotated by C. Leon Harris.

Auditors Office/Annapolis Sept'r. 1818

I certify that it appears by the Pay Roll of the Troops in the Maryland Line that James Due a private Received Arrears of Pay from the 1ˢᵗ of August 1780 to the Nov'r. 1783.

R Loockerman Aud'r Gen'l.[lvii]

4ᵗʰ Judicial District of Maryland

On this 9ᵗʰ day of March 1821 personally appears in open court in the county Court of Caroline County, in the 4ᵗʰ Judicial District in the State of Maryland being a Court of record, constituted by the laws of this State a Court of Common Law, with civil and criminal Jurisdiction to an unlimited extent, James Due aged some more than sixty years, resident in Caroline County in the State of Maryland who being first duly sworn according to law doth on his oath declare and say, that he served in the revolutionary war as follows to wit that he enlisted in the spring of the year 1778 under Captain John Hawkins of Queen Anne County in the State of Maryland for the term of nine months that at the expiration of that time he enlisted for three years and soon after he returned home on furlough, and on his return to the army, he again enlisted for during the wars that he was a little in the rear of the army at the Battle of White Plains (28 Oct,

1776). And was in the Battle at Elizabeth Town and was there taken prisoner by the Refugees and detained more than ten months and that after he again joined the army, he was in several skirmishes and finally in the siege of little York and Capture of the British Army under Lord Cornwallis that he did by a declaration made in Queen Anne's County Court on or about the fourth day of November 188 obtain a certificate of pension No. 5876 and since received his pension to the 4th day of March, 1820.

And I do solemnly swore that he was a resident Citizen of the United States on the 18th day of March, 1818, and that I have not since that time by gift sale or in any manner disposed of my property or any part thereof with intent thereby so to diminish it as to bring myself within the provisions of an act of Congress entitled "an act to provide for certain persons engaged in the land and naval service of the United States in the Revolutionary War" passed on the 18th day of March 1818 and that I have not nor has any person in trust for me any property or securities contracts or debts due to me nor have I any income other than what is contained in the Schedule hereto annexed and by me subscribed to wit.15 acres of poor sandy Land,- 6 horned cattle of different ages, 8 hogs, 2 cupboards and some Cupboard ware -2 tables- 6 Chairs, some articles of Iron & wooden ware - 1 old horse Cart (small) -1 old plough & Harrow (very ordinary) that this deponent owes about the sum of *$41.00* to J. Bradly, F. H. Hawley, H. Meeds, J. Dyett, D. Casson, R. Cooper & K. Godwin. I am by occupation a country shoemaker and with the increase of years, I experiences the failure of my sight together with his other bodily powers, That I have residing in my family one, woman named Elizabeth Civil, a housekeeper aged about forty years - one son named Enock aged 26 years who works for his own maintenance, one other son named John aged 17 years employed in the tillage of my lot of ground - one daughter named Rachel, aged 17 years, and one daughter named Surrena, aged 12 years both of whom are employed in my family. He signed the declaration of facts with an X mark.

James his X mark Due

NOTE: On 27 April 1822, James Due gave the name of his Colonel as "William Richardson," correctly spelled William Richardson. ("S34771 James Due") A document in the file states that James Due died on 4 Feb 1832.[lviii]

Archives of Maryland Online

Maryland State Archives I Index I Help I Search

Session Laws, 1831

Volume 213, Page 228   View pdf image (33K)   Jump to [page] [▼] [ ] 60   lix

1831	LAWS OF MARYLAND.
CHAP. 175	CHAPTER 174
Passed Mar.3, 1832	An act for the benefit of Enoch Due, John Due and Serena Due, formerly, now Screna Pritchard, by her intermarriage with a certain Samuel Pritchard, natural children of James Due, late of Caroline county, deceased.
Preamble,	WHEREAS, the said James Due departed this life, oft or about the fourth day of February, in the year of our Lord, eighteen hundred and thirty-two, intestate, leaving the said Enoch Due, John Due and Serena Pritchard, his natural children; and, although recognized and owned by the. said James Due, in his life time, to be his children, in consequence of their not being born in Wedlock, the said children cannot, agreeably to law, heir their fathers property— Therefore,
Right in estatate vested.	Be it enacted by the General Assembly of Maryland, That it shall and may be lawful, after all the funeral expenses, and all other just claims against the said James Due's estate, shall have been fully paid and satisfied; that the said Enoch Due, John Due and Serena Pritchard, being the natural children of the said James Due, shall have, hold, possess, and enjoy all and singular the residue of the said James Due's estate, real, personal or mixed, to them and their heirs forever, share and shape alike, any thing in any law, custom, or usage to the contrary not withstanding.

Location of James Due's Property was found in Land Records for Caroline County.

1856/10/16 Grantor: Walter Massey Grantee: John E. Starkey
Parcel: Bradley Farm   Acreage: 369 Lib: No: Fol: CC:263
Type: Deed

Condensed:

Also another tract, this one called Godfreys Folly situate on the East side of Tuckahoe Creek and adjoining the mill [seat] commonly known as Rickett's Mill and also near an old mill called Wooter's Mill: Beginning at a boundary tree being the beginning tree of a tract called New Beckley situated on the South side of the branch of the old mill pond called Wooters which said tract was purchased by John Bradley, deceased, of John Due, Samuel Pritchett and Sarena A. Pritchett, heirs of James Due, deceased, containing ten acres ... All of which tracts constitute the Bradley Farm, being the same conveyed to the aforesaid Abraham Gump, deceased, by Richard N. Potter, trustee for the sale of the real estate of the above-named John Bradley recorded by a deed dated May 11, 1844. Said lands have three hundred and sixty-nine acres. Witnesses: Justice of the Peace James B. Steele, Junior and Thomas F. Gary, Caroline County clerk. lx

Serena Due, Oliver Downes Sr.'s third great-grandmother, was born outside of marriage and faced the social stigma associated with it. Her racial physical characteristics and those of her brother Enoch suggest they were Caucasian, but there is no information available about her other siblings, John and Rachael. Although James Due, her father, was described as a Black person by census takers for several decades, it is unclear if he was multiracial. It is assumed that Serena's mother was White, as it was illegal for people of color to marry White people at that time. James Due did not indenture his children, but instead employed them on his land and in his shoemaking business. Serena was about eight years older than Frederick Douglass and lived in Hillsboro around the same time as him and his family. Samuel Pritchett, Serena's husband, was an acquaintance of James Due and was himself multiracial, with oral history suggesting he descended from White Pritchetts and/or had Native American ancestry. Oliver and his African American Pritchett cousins' DNA testing did not match with White descendants of Dr. John Pritchett's lineage, who were the White Pritchetts' progenitors in Dorchester County, Maryland, suggesting that Samuel did not descend from them. It is possible that Samuel descended from a White female Pritchard, but until more direct male Pritchetts do DNA testing, the mystery remains unsolved. Samuel was about forty-one years old when he married sixteen-year-old Serena in 1826. Serena's mother's name is unknown, but in 1818, a woman named Elizabeth Cevil lived with James Due and his children. However, there is no evidence that she is the mother of any of James Due's children. All of James's children were born out of wedlock, and interracial marriage had been illegal since 1692 for free Black and White people. Serena gave birth to her first son, George, at the age of seventeen, according to this first volume. Samuel was not a farmer and did not own any land but worked as a laborer. James Due's death in 1832 notes that Serena was married to Samuel Pritchard at the time. The next son, Medford Pritchett, was born in 1833 after the events in this volume, but it is possible that Serena had other children who died in infancy or became unknown adults. It is also possible that Samuel had a previous family about which there is no information. During the research of Samuel and Serena's lineage, it was discovered that Oliver Downes Sr. and his siblings share DNA with descendants of Owen Stanley and Harriet Wharton, a topic that will be explored in volume two, along with further information about Serena and Samuel Pritchett's lives.

Tidbit: According to Andrew Dhue, the descendants of Enoch Dhue and his children had a distinct Scottish Gaelic accent, but it is unclear whether this was due to James Due or Enoch's mother. Further research is needed to determine the source of this accent. In 2019, the author was inducted into the Daughters of the American Revolution based on the African American Patriot James Due, while cousins Dean Henry and Gerald Scott were inducted into the Sons of the American Revolution. In 2021, the author and Dean Henry were inducted into the Society of First African Families of English America under James Due. The Society of the First African Families of English America is a lineage organization that unites descendants of African ancestry who lived in English America prior to March 5, 1770 the date of the Boston Massacre and the death of Crispus Attucks the first patriot casualty of the American Revolution.

"I would unite with anybody to do right and with nobody to do wrong."

- Frederick Douglass

Anti-slavery Movement: A Lecture

Chapter 10

Timeline of Oliver Downes Sr.'s Ancestors and Surrounding Neighbors

1632 The Province of Maryland also known as the Maryland Colony was founded in 1632 as a haven for English Catholics fleeing anti-Catholic persecution in Europe. But many of the original settlers were Protestants.

1660 Maryland legalized slavery of Africans.

1664 Maryland Colony passed law declaring that all "Negroes or other slaves," whether already in the province, or to be imported later, were to serve for life. All children born of any Black or other slave were to be "Slaves as their fathers." It also stipulated that White woman who married slaves would be declared slaves and their children will also be slaves. To further discourage such marriages, the children of matches contracted after the act's passage were to be "Slaves as their fathers were." The children of such marriages contracted before the act's passage were to serve their parents' slaveholders until they reached the age of thirty-one.[lxi]

1665 Maternal eighth great-grandmother, **Maudlin Magee,** Born ABT. 1665, in Belfast, Northern Ireland, United Kingdom.

1669 Dorchester County settled by whites, free Blacks, and enslaved Africans.

1670 Maternal eighth great-grandfather, **Sambo Game,** Born in Africa Death 1734 in Virginia, USA. Voting restricted by the Governor to planters with 50-acre freehold or property worth 40 pounds; officeholding restricted to owners of 1,000 acres.

1672 The Royal African Company was given sole monopoly to import African slaves to the Americas.

1681 In the past slaveholders forced marriages between White women and the enslaved Negroes no doubt to get more service from White women and to procure more slaves, perhaps in compensation for the scarcity of Black females. To end such abuses, the law imposed a fine of 10,000 pounds of tobacco upon any slaveholder whom a court of law found guilty of forcing a mixed marriage and a similar fine upon any official solemnizing such a match. Furthermore, any woman so forced was to be freed and any children resulting from the marriage were to be exempt from the paternal descent clause. The husband remained a slave and the marriage, albeit not one of choice, remained intact.[lxii]

1687 Maternal seventh great-grandmother, **Fortune Game Magee,** was born.

1692 Maryland enacted a law that punished White women who had children by slaves by selling them as servants for seven years and binding their children to serve until the age of twenty-one if they were married to the slave, and until thirty-one if they were not married. Any non-servant freeborn White woman who married a Black man was to become a servant of her church parish for seven years. Her husband, if free, was to become a slave for the parish. The same penalties befalling a White woman as detailed above were to apply to any White man begetting any Black woman with child. [lxiii]

1695 New act said that no Black slave whatsoever shall presume at any time to travel to any place of meeting or resort to wander about from Plantation to Plantation under pretext of visiting. Slave holders were to issue written passes to any slave who traveled abroad on legitimate business or be fined two hundred pounds of tobacco. [lxiv]

1698 Monopoly of slave trade by Royal African Company abolished by Parliament; slave imports markedly increase.

1699 New Act, multiracial children were to serve for thirty-one years instead of twenty-one, and free Black men fathering multiracial children had their punishment reduced from life servitude to seven years.

1700 Paternal fifth great-grandfather, **Thomas Wyatt,** was born in Queen Anne's, Maryland.

1705 Virginia classified non-reservation Indians as "free people of color."

1706 January 17, Benjamin Franklin was born.

1715 Maternal sixth great-grandmother, **Sarah Fortune,** was born. The New Act said that no servant (slaves not specified) was to wander beyond ten miles from his or her slave holder/master's house without a pass signed by their owner. Any person harboring "any such Servant or Slave" (first mention of slaves) was to be fined five hundred pounds of tobacco for every night or 24-hour period. Any free Black or multiracial person harboring a runaway was to be fined double and be subjected to servitude if he or she could not pay. Any person traveling outside his or her county without a pass from their home county justices was subject to seizure as a runaway servant. Any person who seized a runaway servant or slave could use the fugitive as he or she saw fit until the next county court session. were limited to ten lashes when correcting servants (slaves not specified) and were enjoined from otherwise mistreating them. All African Americans would be slaves during their natural lives. Baptism of Black people would not be grounds for freedom. Ministers, pastors, or magistrates who solemnized marriages between Black people or multiracial people and Whites were fined five thousand pounds of tobacco. Any free Black person or multiracial person marrying a White was to become a slave for life, except multiracial people born of White women, who were to become servants for seven years. Whites so marrying were to become servants for seven years.[lxv]

1717 New Act made a free Black person or multiracial person, except multiracial people born of White women, slaves for life.[lxvi]

1723 New Act Slaveholders allowing slaves to own livestock were to be fined five hundred pounds tobacco. The contraband livestock was to be confiscated and its value divided between the province and the informer. Runaway and outlying Black people could be shot to death upon refusal to surrender.[lxvii]

1724 New Act All Blacks, or other slaves convicted by a jury or upon confession of housebreaking, petty treason, or murder could be punished thus, "to have the Right Hand cut off, to be Hanged in the usual manner, the Head severed from the Body, the Body divided into Four Quarters, and Head and Quarters set up, in the most public Places."[lxviii]

1729 A ship from Montrose has lately gone up the bay carrying sixty indentured Scots.[lxix]

1744 Native-American chiefs of the Six Nations relinquished by treaty all claims to land in colony. Assembly purchased last Indian land claims in Maryland.

1745 Maternal 5th great-grandfather, **Humphrey Fortune,** born in Essex County, Virginia.

1746 Frederick Douglass's great-grandmother, Jenny, was born enslaved on the property of Richard Skinner, a tobacco planter in the Miles River Neck district of the Eastern Shore's Talbot County. A man named Bailey who was enslaved with her could been Jenny's father. Jenny went by Bailey before she married her husband who was also named Bailey.

1747 The African descent Gibbs family were left 444 acres in Queen Anne's County by the will of their slaveholder.[lxx]

1758 Paternal fourth great-grandfather, **James Due,** was born between 1748-1758.

1759 John Champe & Company say that Captain William Rice, in the Ship *True Blue*, has just arrived in Patowmack River from Africa with 350 Gold Coast slaves. Taylor & Ritchie say they have slaves for sale that just arrived from Gambia. Captain Thomas Birch arrived in Annapolis from Gambia in the ship *Upton* with over two hundred slaves.[lxxi]

1760 Possible paternal fourth great-grandfather, **Noah Wyatt,** was born in Maryland.

1761 Thomas Ringgold, William Ringgold, and Samuel Galloway will sell slaves at Annapolis on 4 August 1761, imported from Africa by Captain Neilson in the *Snow Alexander*[lxxii]

1767 John Due charged fornication with Sarah Barnet. Several unmarried women with children had no support. They usually end up in court asking for aid. The county courts would charge the unwed women with fornication to find the father (if named or could be found) to support both the woman and child involved.[lxxiii]

1768 Ann Pritchard charged for fornication-had mulatto child.[lxxiv] Quakers in Maryland no longer buy or sell slaves.

1769 Maryland merchants adopted policy of nonimportation of British goods.

1770 Paternal 4th great-grandfather, **John Cooper,** was born. **Crispus Attackus**, an American whaler, sailor, and stevedore of African and Native American descent, regarded as the first person killed in the Boston Massacre and thus the first American killed in the American Revolution.

1773 James Due was between 25 and 15 years of age when the Boston Tea Party occurred.

1774 Maryland ended the international slave trade.

1775 The start of the American Revolutionary War, the conflict between Great Britain and the Thirteen Colonies.

1776 Paternal 4th great-grandmother **Lydia Talbot** was born in Maryland. The 5th Maryland Regiment was composed of eight companies from Queen Anne, Kent, Caroline, and Dorchester Counties. On July 4, 1776, the United States Declaration of Independence was signed by the delegates of the Continental Congress in Philadelphia, and Maryland declared itself a sovereign state. The Constitution of 1776 granted the right to vote for all freemen who were of age and who held a certain amount of property.

General Washington authorized the enlistment of free Black people with prior military experience in January 1776, and in January 1777, he extended the terms to all free Black people to help fill the depleted ranks of the Continental Army. Because the states frequently failed to meet their quotas for the army, Congress authorized the enlistment of all Black people, whether free or enslaved, in 1777. On September 9, 1776, the Continental Congress officially declared the name of the new nation to be the "United States" of America.

1778 **Polly Fortune**, who is Oliver Downes Sr.'s maternal fourth great-grandmother, was born in Virginia. Maryland was the seventh state to join the United States. In the spring of 1778, James Due, Oliver's fourth great-grandfather, enlisted in Queen Anne's County, Maryland, as a private in Captain John Hawkins' company of the 5th Maryland Regiment. He fought in the Battle of Elizabethtown where he was captured and held prisoner for around eleven months. He returned to the army and fought in the Siege of Yorktown. According to a document called "Return of the Negroes in the Army" dated August 24, 1778, there were approximately ninety-five "Negroes" among the Maryland troops.

1779 Edward Lloyd (1779-1834), the Governor of Maryland, 1809-11, born at "Wye House," near Easton.

1780 Maternal third great-grandfather, **Major Acree**, born in Virginia. Maternal third great-grandmother, **Nancy Carter,** born in Virginia.

1783 Maryland stripped Black people who owned property the right to vote. Maryland also prohibited the importation of slaves. **James Due** was honorably discharged from the Army on November 15, 1783. The war ended.

1785 Paternal third great-grandfather, **Samuel Pritchett,** was born in Maryland. Possible paternal third great-grandfather, **Benjamin Downes,** was born in Maryland.

1786 Maternal third great-grandmother, **Matilda Sparks,** born in Maryland.

1788 Free Blacks in Talbot County formed The Hill Community in Easton.[lxxv]

1790 Paternal third great-grandfather **Josephus Cephas** was born in Maryland. The first United States Federal Census Record was taken under the Secretary of State Thomas Jefferson.

1792 In Maryland, "No negro or mulatto whether born free or manumitted, or made free under any past, present, or future law of this state" could vote in any election. **Frederick Douglas's** mother, **Harriet Bailey,** was born.

1794 Paternal fifth great-grandfather, **Owen Stanley,** was born in Reading, Berkshire, England. Paternal fifth great-grandmother, **Harriet Wharton,** was born in Plymouth, Devon, England.

1800 Maternal third great-grandfather, **Joseph Flamer,** was born in Maryland.

1801 Thomas Jefferson became the third president of the United States. Sally Hemings had a daughter, Harriet, born in May.

1804 Paternal third great-grandmother, **Henrietta Wyatt,** was born in Maryland. Paternal third great-grandfather, **Nathan Arthur Clark,** was born in Maryland.

1805 Maryland prohibited free African Americans from selling and growing staple crops (wheat, corn, and tobacco) without a license.

The General Assembly passed a law Chapter 66 to find free African Americans and to control the availability of freedom papers. The law required African Americans who were born free to record proof of their freedom in the county court. "The court would then issue them a certificate of freedom."[lxxvi] If the African American had been manumitted, the court clerk or register of wills would look up the manumitting document before issuing a certificate of freedom. A typical certificate not only shows how the individual became free, but also lists physical characteristics that could be used to prove identity. These include height, eye color, complexion, and hair color and texture.[lxxvii]

1806 Paternal 3rd great-grandmother, **Mary Cooper,** was born in Maryland. Paternal third great-grandfather, **Joseph Matthews,** was born in Maryland.

1807 Thomas Jefferson signs the act prohibiting the importation of slaves from outside the United States. But did not end domestic slave trading.

1808 Maternal 3rd great-grandfather, **Taliaferro Fortune,** born in Virginia. The General Assembly passed new legislation that specifically empowered county courts to apprentice free Black children. Children of "lazy and worthless free negroes" could be bound to eligible White masters. Ten years later, the legislature revised the apprentice law to encourage the courts to consult with parents before removing a child from his or her home.[lxxviii] The U.S. Congressional Act Prohibiting Importation of Slaves takes effect. More than 400,000 slaves have been brought into the country from Africa. There are now one million slaves living in the United States. The US is the only country where there is a natural increase in the enslaved population.

1809 Edward Lloyd V is the governor of Maryland. James Madison is the fourth president of the United States.

1810 Paternal 3rd great-grandmother, **Serena Due,** was born in Caroline County, Maryland. The congress amended the constitution that voting rights was limited to White men only. Free Blacks disenfranchised.

1812 The United States declared war on Britain. At the war's end three to five thousand Black men, women and children from Maryland and Virginia received their freedom from the British. Some were sent to Bermuda, Trinidad, Nova Scotia, and New Brunswick.[lxxix]

1813 Frederick Douglass's oldest brother, **Perry Downs,** was born in Maryland.

1814 Maternal 2nd great-grandfather, **John Sparks,** born in Maryland.

1815 Maternal 2nd great-grandmother, **Loretta Turner,** born in Maryland.

1816 Daniel Coker and other Black church leaders formed independent African Methodist Episcopal (AME) Church is founded in Philadelphia, Pennsylvania. It is originally formed of 16 African American congregations that band together. It emphasized education of Black people. It was also an anti-slavery abolitionist group. Served as a station of the Underground Railroad.

1817 James Monroe was the fifth president of the United States. Abraham Dobson, who owned a flock of twenty-six sheep in 1817, was also one of the wealthiest freedmen in Talbot County.[lxxx]

1818 Frederick Douglass was born into slavery as Frederick Augustus Washington Bailey on the Eastern Shore Maryland.

1819 Paternal 2nd great-grandfather, **Joseph Cephas,** was born in Maryland.

1820 Joseph Matthews and **Henrietta Wyatt's** daughter, **Henrietta,** was born in Caroline, Maryland. Maternal second great-grandfather, **Matthew Johns,** born in Maryland. President James Monroe signed order banning Black people or multiracial people from serving in the U.S. Army.

1822 Araminta "Minty" Ross, later known as **Harriet Tubman**, was born enslaved in Dorchester County.

1825 John Quincy Adams was the sixth president of the United States.

1826 Maternal 2nd great-grandfather, **Ruffin Acree,** was born about 1826 in King and Queen County, Virginia.

1827 Samuel Pritchett and **Serena Due's** son, **George W Pritchett,** was born in 1827 in Caroline, Maryland.

1829 Andrew Jackson was the seventh president of the United States.

1830 second paternal great-grandfather, **Wilson Downes,** was born in Maryland. Second maternal great-grandmother, **Mary J Homer** was born in Maryland.

1831 Maternal 2nd great-grandmother, **Peggy Ann Fortune,** was born about 1831 in King and Queen County, Virginia. The Underground Railroad became the name of the network that helped the enslaved escape to freedom. It was engineered by Black and

White abolitionists. Maryland responded to Nat Turner's rebellion by drafting a new, more comprehensive law, further curtailing slaves' privileges and usurping the rights of free Black people. Maryland prohibited free Black people from carrying arms and further prohibited free African Americans from selling bacon, beef, pork, oats, and rye without a license from a justice of the peace. Anyone who bought these products from an unlicensed African American faced prosecution for receiving stolen goods. All people of color were forbidden to assemble or to attend meetings for religious purposes which were not conducted by a White licensed clergyman or by some respectable White of the neighborhood authorized by the clergyman.[lxxxi]

1832 On February 4th, **James Due** (fourth great grandfather) died in Hillsboro Maryland. Andrew Jackson was president. In aftermath of Nat Turner rebellion in Virginia, Maryland laws enacted to restrict free Blacks.

AFTERWORD

The importance of understanding our ancestral stories goes beyond just names and dates on a chart. With the help of DNA tests, oral history, and available sources, we can reconstruct our ancestors' lives and legacies. As Beth Pruitt stated in her dissertation *Reordering the Landscape: Science, Nature, And Spirituality at Wye House,* "Unlike Frederick Douglass, these are the names of people who did not write their histories down, but instead left their legacy on the ground, in objects, and with the present-day descendants in nearby towns. They were the people that Douglass lived with and wrote about."[lxxxii]

Although Oliver Downes Sr.'s ancestors did not leave written records of their lives, their legacies can still be felt through their present-day descendants in nearby towns. While this volume has provided some insight into the life of James Due, it is important to seek out additional resources to fully understand the experiences of African Americans during this time period. One recommendation is to read the autobiographies of Frederick Douglass, which provide a first-hand account of life on the Eastern Shore. Additionally, John Muller's book, "Frederick Douglass in Washington, D.C.: The Lion of Anacostia," is highly recommended for its research on Douglass's later years. The second volume will include more information about Frederick Douglass's life. It is hoped that this volume will be helpful for fellow researchers to continue delving deeper into their ancestors' lives.

Images

Cover:
https://www.loc.gov/pictures/item/2006679024/ *African American woman doing laundry with a scrub board and tub, African American girl stirring pot with 3 other children on the ground watching, and a woman in the background spreading laundry.* January 4, 2022. Print. Library of Congress Prints and Photographs Division Washington, D.C. 20540 USA

Miller, Stephani Juleeana. Photograph of Oliver Downes January 4, 2022. Author's personal collection.

Miller, Stephani Juleeana. Photograph of Edwina Downes January 4, 2022. Author's personal collection.

Miller, Stephani Juleeana. Photograph of Rosalie Downes January 4, 2022. Author's personal collection.

Miller, Stephani Juleeana. Photograph of Vella Downes January 4, 2022. Author's personal collection.

Miller, Stephani Juleeana. Photograph of Avis Schwartz January 4, 2022. Author's personal collection.

Johnston, Frances Benjamin. Port Tobacco Houses, Port Tobacco, Charles County, Maryland. January 4, 2022. Print. Library of Congress Prints and Photographs Division Washington, D.C. 20540 USA. https://www.loc.gov/pictures/item/2017887444/

Reference Notes

Chapter 1

[i] (23andme.com 2021)

Chapter 2

[ii] (Dorsey 2012)
[iii] (Hawass 2012)
[iv] (Geni 2022)
[v] (Simms TM 2011 Dec;146(4))
[vi] (Sherbondy 2021)
[vii] (Pruitt 2022)

Chapter 3

[viii] (Bogen Spring 2001)
[ix] (Bogen Spring 2001)
[x] (Zug-Gilbert 2001)
[xi] (Douglass 2018)

Chapter 4

[xii] (J. L. Douglas 2005)
[xiii] (Faragher 1996)
[xiv] (Woodtor 1999)
[xv] (Preston 1980. 2018)
[xvi] (Douglass 2018)
[xvii] (Douglass 2018)
[xviii] (Preston 1980. 2018)

Chapter 5

[xix] (Maryland State Archives 2019)
[xx] (Maryland State Archives 2019)
[xxi] (Wood 2019)
[xxii] (Salinger 1987)
[xxiii] (J. L. Douglas 2005)
[xxiv] (Russ n.d.)
[xxv] (Historic Sites Consortium of Queen Anne's County 2001-2022)

[xxvi] (Preston 1980. 2018)
[xxvii] (Douglass, My Bondage and My Freedom 2003)
[xxviii] (Preston 1980. 2018)
[xxix] (Preston 1980. 2018)
(Contributed for use in USGenWeb Archives by Cathy Downes 2000)
[xxxi] (J. L. Douglas 2005)
[xxxii] (J. L. Douglas 2005)
[xxxiii] (Pioneer 1878)
[xxxiv] (Fought 2017)
[xxxv] (Contributed for use in USGenWeb Archives by Cathy Downes 2000)
[xxxvii] (Queen Anne County Judgment Records n.d.) The old Queen Anne County judgement record books are stored at the Maryland Archives in Annapolis. And are in poor condition.
[xxxviii] (Carothers, Maryland Oaths Of Fidelity 1989, 1995)

Chapter 6

[xxxix] (Wilkinson 2020, 39)
[xl] (Williamson 1980)
[xli] (Preston 1980. 2018)
[xlii] (Heinegg 2001)
[xliii] (Krech III 1981)
[xliv]

Chapter 7

[xlv] (Mark 2021)
[xlvi] (Mitsawokett 1997-2022)
[xlvii] (Rarihokwats 1998)

Chapter 8

[xlviii] (Woodtor 1999)
[xlix] (Dorsey 2012)
[l] (Wikipedia contributors 2022)
[li] (Archives 2007)
[lii] (IBW21 2018)
[liii] (Wikipedia contributors 2022)
[liv] (Hynson 1998)
[lv] (Meyer 2001)

Chapter 9

[lvi] (National Society Daughters Of The American Revolution 2008)

[lvii] (Harris n.d.)
[lviii] (Harris n.d.)
[lix] (Maryland State Archives 2018)
[lx] (Langford 2010)

Chapter 10

[lxi] (Maryland State Archives 2000)
[lxii] (Maryland State Archives 2000)
[lxiii] (Maryland State Archives 2000)
[lxiv] (Maryland State Archives 2000)
[lxv] (Maryland State Archives 2000)
[lxvi] (Maryland State Archives 2000)
[lxvii] (Maryland State Archives 2000)
[lxviii] (Maryland State Archives 2000)
[lxix] (Green 1980, 4)
[lxx] (Hynson 1998)
[lxxi] (Green 1980, 231)
[lxxii] (Green 1980, 271)
[lxxiii] (Queen Anne County Judgment Records n.d.)
[lxxiv] (Queen Anne County Judgment Records n.d.)
[lxxv] (THE HILL COMMUNITY 2019)
[lxxvi] (Maryland State Archives 2000)
[lxxvii] (Maryland State Archives 2018)
[lxxviii] (Maryland State Archives 2018)
[lxxix] (Archives 2007)
[lxxx] (Dorsey 2012)
[lxxxi] (Free Blacks in Maryland 2016)

Afterward

[lxxxii] (E. Pruitt 2015)

Works Cited Page

National Society Daughters Of The American Revolution . 2008. *Forgotten Patriots : African American And American Indian Patriots In The Revolutionary War , A Guide to Service, Sources and Studies.* Washington D.C.: The DAR Store.

23andme.com. 2021. *Ancestry Timeline of Edwina's.* July 23. Accessed November 20, 2022.

Archives, Annapolis MD The Maryland State. 2007. "A Guide to the History in Maryland." *Maryland State Archives.* January 1. Accessed February 3, 2020. http://slavery.msa.maryland.gov/pdf/md-slavery-guide-2020.pdf.

Bogen, David S. Spring 2001. "Mathius de Sousa; Maryland's First Colonist of African Descent." *Maryland Historical Magazine 96 (1)* 68-85.

Carothers, Bettie. 1989, 1995. *Maryland Oaths Of Fidelity.* Westminister: Family Line P.

Dorsey, Jennifer Hull. 2012. *Hirelings:African American Workers and Free labor in Early Maryland.* Cornell University Press. Kindle Edition.

Douglas, Joseph L. 2005. *Perry Bailey a.k.a. Downs and Samuel A. Douglas: Relatives Of Frederick Douglass A Family History (1733-1929).* Bountiful: Family History Publishers.

Douglass, Frederick. 2003. *My Bondage and My Freedom.* New York: Penguin Books.

—. 2018. *Narrative of the Life of Frederick Douglass, an American Slave.* Madison & Adams Press.

Faragher, John Mack. 1996. *The Encyclopedia of Colonial and Revolutionary America.* New York: Da Capo Press.

Fought, Leigh. 2017. *Women in the World of Frederick Douglass.* New York: Oxford University Press.

2016 . "Free Blacks in Maryland." *Maryland AHGP.* February 11. Accessed November 20, 2022. https://mdahgp.genealogyvillage.com/free_blacks_in_maryland.html.

Geni. 2022. "E-M34 (Y-DNA)." *Geni.* Accessed November 20, 2022. https://www.geni.com/projects/E-M34-Y-DNA/8402#:~:text=E-M34%20is%20prevalent%20among%20Ashkenazi%20and%20Sephardic%20Jews%2C,throughout%20western%20Asia%20and%20Europe%20from%20the%20Levant.

Geni.com. 2022. *E-M34 (Y-DNA).* Accessed January 1, 2021. https://www.geni.com/projects/E-M34-Y-DNA/8402#:~:text=E-M34%20is%20prevalent%20among%20Ashkenazi%20and%20Sephardic%20Jews%2C,throughout%20western%20Asia%20and%20Europe%20from%20the%20Levant.

Green, Karen Mauer. 1980. *The Maryland Gazette 1727-1761.* Galveston: The Frontier Press.

Harris, C. Leon. n.d. "Pension Application of James Due S34771 MD." *Southern Campaigns American Revolution Pension Statements and Rosters.* Accessed November 20, 2022. https://revwarapps.org/s34771.pdf.

Hawass, Z et al. 2012. "Revising the harem conspiracy and death of Ramessess III: anthropological, forensic, radiological, and genetic study." *BMJ 345* https://www.bmj.com/content/345/bmj.e8268.

Heinegg, Paul. 2001. *Free African Americans of Maryland and Delaware from the Colonial Period to 1810.* Madison: Clearfield.

Historic Sites Consortium of Queen Anne's County. 2001-2022. *Old Wye Mill.* Accessed November 20, 2022.

https://historicqac.org/historic-site/old-wye-mill/#:~:text=During%20the%20American%20Revolution%2C%20the%20Wye%20Grist%20Mill,the%20Eastern%20Shore%20the%20%E2%80%9CBreadbasket%20of%20the%20Revolution.%E2%80%9D.

Hynson, Jerry M. 1998. *Free Africans-Americans of Maryland 1832.* Westminister: Heritage Books.

IBW21. 2018. "The Eastern Shore of Maryland is the birthplace of many black revolutionaries. Why?" *ibw21.org.* September 7. Accessed November 20, 2022. https://ibw21.org/commentary/the-eastern-shore-of-maryland-is-the-birthplace-of-many-black-revolutionaries-why/.

Krech III, Shepardd. 1981. *Praise The Bridge That Carries You Over The Life Of Joseph Sutton.* Cambridge: Schenkman Publishing Co,.

Landis-Smith, Donna. 2016. "Downes Warren family to be honored at fair." *MyEasternshoreMD.* August 3. Accessed November 20, 2022. https://www.myeasternshoremd.com/breaking/downes-warren-family-to-be-honored-at-fair/article_b0f6d35e-fd37-50d3-bbb2-bae74061a6ac.html.

Langford, Cullen G and Langford George III. 2010. "Massey Land Records 1673-1867 for Caroline County, Maryland." *Massey Land Records 1673-1867 for Caroline County, Maryland.* Accessed November 20, 2022. https://www.georgesbasement.com/LangfordOnMassey/MasseyDataBank/MasseyLandRecordsCarolineCountyMaryland10102012.htm.

LibreTexts. 2019. "Fighting Their Way to Freedom." *LibreTexts Humanities.* September 19. Accessed November 20, 2022. https://human.libretexts.org/Courses/Achieving_the_Dream/Book%3A_African_American_History_and_Culture/04%3A_African_Americans_and_the_American_Revolution/04.3%3A_Fighting_Their_Way_to_Freedom.

Mark, Joshua J. 2021. "Powhatan Confederacy." *World History Encyclopedia.* March 1. Accessed November 20, 2022. https://www.worldhistory.org/Powhatan_Confederacy/.

Maryland State Archives. 2018. "1831 Laws of Maryland Chapter 174." *Archives of Maryland .* August 2. Accessed 2022. https://msa.maryland.gov/megafile/msa/speccol/sc2900/sc2908/000001/000213/html/am213--228.html.

—. 2018. *Archives of Maryland online.* August 2. Accessed July 10, 2020. https://msa.maryland.gov/megafile/msa/speccol/sc2900/sc2908/000001/000836/html/index.html.

—. 2000. "BLACKS BEFORE THE LAW IN COLONIAL MARYLAND Chapter III FREEDOM OR BONDAGE -- THE LEGISLATIVE RECORD." *Maryland State Archives.* November 14. Accessed November 20, 2022. https://msa.maryland.gov/msa/speccol/sc5300/sc5348/html/chap3.html.

Meyer, Mary K. 2001. *Free Blacks in Harford, Somerset and Talbot Counties, Maryland.* Goshen: Willow Bend Books.

Mitsawokett. 1997-2022. *Mitsawokett.* Accessed November 20, 2022. https://nativeamericansofdelawarestate.com/MainMenu.html.

Pioneer, West-Jersey. 1878. "Chronicling America: Historic American Newspapers." *Library of Congress.* September 19. Accessed November 20, 2022. https://chroniclingamerica.loc.gov/lccn/sn83032103/1878-09-19/ed-1/seq-2/?fbclid=IwAR3TNwxhRhyn0-gWKTamOlCp9IhrXAi_e5naL6Th2LXap2IkXb9oBMf2ysU.

Preston, Dickson J. 1980. 2018. *Young Frederick Douglass: The Maryland Years.* Baltimore: John Hopkins University Press.

Pruitt, Elizabeth. 2015. *Reordering the Landscape: Science, Nature, and Spirituality at Wye House.* Accessed March 3, 2021. http://hdl.handle.net/1903/16675.

Pruitt, Sarah. 2022. *Who are the Mandinka? Find out more about the Mali descendants.* May 31. Accessed June 10, 2022. https://www.history.com/news/who-are-the-mandinka.

n.d. *Queen Anne County Judgment Records.* Annapolis : Maryland Archives,.

Rarihokwats, R. 1998. "Lee/Leroy Acree, son of Ruffin & Peggy." *Genealogy.com.* December 25. Accessed November 20, 2022. https://www.genealogy.com/forum/surnames/topics/acree/26/.

Russ, Jean B. n.d. *Lloyd, Edward III (1711-1770).* Accessed March 3, 2021. https://msa.maryland.gov/megafile/msa/speccol/sc3500/sc3520/000800/000810/html/ndnbelloyd3.html.

Salinger, Sharon V. 1987. *To Serve Well and Faithfully: Labor and Indentured Servants in Pennsylvania, 1682-1800.* Cambridge: Cambridge University.

Sherbondy, Jeanette. 2021. *Slavery and Tobacco .* August 3. Accessed January 15, 2022. https://www.commonsenseeasternshore.org/slaves-for-tobacco .

Simms TM, Martinez E, Herrera KJ, Wright MR, Perez OA, Hernandez M, Ramirez EC, McCartney Q, Herrera RJ,. 2011 Dec;146(4). "Paternal lineages signal distinct genetic contributions from British Loyalists and continental Africans among different Bahamian Islands." *Am J Phys Anthropol.* 594-608 .

2019. "THE HILL COMMUNITY." *The Hill Community Project.* Accessed November 20, 2022. https://thehillcommunityproject.org/ .

Wikipedia contributors. 2022. "Anthony Johnson (colonist)." *Wikipedia, The Free Encyclopedia.* November 21. Accessed November 21, 2022. https://en.wikipedia.org/w/index.php?title=Anthony_Johnson_(colonist)&oldid=1123073606.

—. 2022. "Republic of Maryland." *Wikipedia, The Free Encyclopedia.* September 15. Accessed November 20, 2022. https://en.wikipedia.org/w/index.php?title=Republic_of_Maryl and&oldid=1110378852.

Wilkinson, A. B. 2020. *Blurring the Lines of Race & Freedom.* Chapel Hill: The University of North Carolina Press.

Williamson, Joel. 1980. *New People: Miscegenation and Mulattoes in the United States.* New York: The Free Press.

Wood, Gregory. Guidry, R. Martin. Rundquist, Marie. 2019. *Acadians were here.* Accessed 15 2021, March. https://acadianswerehere.org/index.html.

Woodtor, Dee Palmer. 1999. *Finding a Place Called Home: A Guide to African-American Genealogy and Hitorical Identity.* New York: Random House.

Zug-Gilbert, Wendy. 2001. "Inventory No. Car-350." *Maryland Historical Trust Maryland Inventory of Historic Properties Fprm.* July.

ABOUT THE AUTHOR

Stephani Miller is a passionate advocate for women's and disability rights, civil liberties, and family history. She possesses more than three decades of nursing experience and has served as CEO of her own company providing Life Coaches and Direct Support Professionals for over twenty years.

Stephani has been a genealogist for over 22 years, specializing in non-paternity events and adoption cases.

In her volunteer work, she serves as the Vice President of Keep It Simple Saints Ministry, a non-profit organization that empowers girls and women in her community. She also holds leadership positions in the Society of the First African Families of English America, National Society Daughters of the Union 1861-1865, and the Daughters of the American Revolution. Additionally, she is a member of the Afro-American Historical and Genealogical Society and the National Genealogical Society.

Stephani has been married for 38 years and is proud of her role as a wife, mother of two sons, and grandmother. She takes pleasure in traveling and participating in family gatherings.

www.ingramcontent.com/pod-product-compliance
Lightning Source LLC
Chambersburg PA
CBHW040129270326
41927CB00004B/93